Also by Cathy Lee Phillips

<u>Silver in the Slop and Other Surprises</u>
(How God puts the "Extra" in the "Ordinary")

D1125501

Speaking of <u>Silver in the Slop</u> . . .

"My daughter and I must have seen ourselves through the pages because we sure did a lot of laughing. I figure any book that can hold my daughter's attention must be a good book!" (Wichita, Kansas)

"I have been reading your book this morning and have tears running down my face from both the laughter and the sweet, sweet sadness conveyed in this book. I intend to share your stories with others . . . ." (Norcross, Georgia)

"Thank you for being such an inspiration. Your book has made me look for the good in all situations." (Knoxville, Tennessee)

"Silver in the Slop is easy for busy people to read because each selection is short enough to read as a break between chores – and the spiritual lessons are a quick pick-me-up." (Greenville, South Carolina)

"I have read the book through but keep it beside my bed and when times get rough I pick it up and read about how God directs certain people into our lives just when we need them most." (Lawrenceville, Georgia)

"This is a book to be read slowly, very slowly, relishing each line, then reflecting for a couple of days on each of the readings. That's how I am reading Silver, and that's how I would recommend other folks read this masterpiece." (Nashville, Tennessee)

Gutsy Little Flowers

Cathy Lee Phillips

Patchwork Press, Ltd.
P. O. Box 4684
Canton, Georgia 30115
www. patchworkpress.com

Gutsy Little Flowers

Copyright © 2001
Patchwork Press
First Printing 2001

Library of Congress Control Number: 2001119431

Scripture Verses are from the King James Version.

Published by:
Patchwork Press
P. O. Box 4684
Canton, Georgia 30115
www. patchworkpress.com

ISBN 0-9715925-1-9

Printed in the USA by

MP

Morris Publishing
3212 East Highway 30 – Kearney, NE 68847 – 1-800-650-7888

Dedicated to

Jim Turner

For the friendship we have shared since 1976.
Here's to LC, late-night term papers, truck stop dinners,
practical jokes, birthday parties, boondoggles,
holidays on the beach, long philosophical conversations,
and too many visits to hospitals --
the latest being my unfortunate toe incident.
I am especially proud of the look of surprise on your face
as you jumped 10 feet in the air one night in Hilton Head.
Gotcha!
Thank you for helping me when I needed it and,
on more than a few times, when I didn't know I needed it.
Thank you for your calm strength and cool head
in moments of turmoil
and, most especially, for your
quiet, gentle ministry of encouragement.

Not bad for a mere Magna!

"Chicken in the bread pan
pickin' out dough!"

--CLP

Table of Contents

v

Section Two: Blossoming

Foreword

When I met Cathy Lee Phillips, she was a freshman at LaGrange College where we became close friends. She took the college by storm with her outstanding sense of humor, musical talent and her outgoing personality. She sings like an angel, plays a "mean" guitar, tells captivating stories, has a streak of mischievousness about her, and graduated Summa cum Laude with a basket-load of honors to go along with that one. I knew at an early age she was destined for greatness and that it would be through her writing. Receiving a note or letter from her is like opening a golden box filled with beautiful treasures. Indeed, her words are an experience. Cathy writes from the realness of her life: joys, pain, strengths, and struggles.

I could not wait for her first book to arrive. When Silver in the Slop was published, I grabbed a copy, took it to my favorite chair and read it from cover to cover. Though it has been over 25 years since I have been to her home in Newnan, Georgia, where so many of the stories took place, I felt I was right there taking the journey with her. I could see the house, the barnyard, the fields, the people, and the animals. I could smell the scents of cattle and pigs and freshly-cut hay. The aroma of home-cooked meals and barbeque filtered through the pages, as did the prickly feel of leaning on the rustic fence looking at the silver in the pig's slop.

When Cathy wrote of her old schoolroom, I could step back in time and relive the sights and sounds of my own boyhood classroom, remembering the smell of chalkboards and hearing erasers rubbing the boards clean. Many things came alive to me that had been buried for years in my memory. I blushed at the story of her buying her first bra, yet easily translated that story into my own struggles that came with puberty. Cathy has an exceptional ability to help the reader experience every sense along the way in the stories she seeks to convey.

Cathy can have me laughing one minute and then quickly turn my emotion into tears streaming down my face. All of her writing has a common thread that runs throughout: each is like a parable and metaphor filled with a greater message than that of the written word. Through her work I am not only able to encounter the people and places about which she writes, but I am able to step into the stories and see myself! Even more amazingly, I am able to encounter that which is greater than myself, for she weaves the greater story of the Christian faith where, suddenly and mysteriously, we experience truth and grace . . . indeed, the living God.

Cathy's life has been filled with a diversity of experience, from a humble home life as a child to being a pastor's wife to experiencing the heart transplant and death of her husband to becoming a widow at a young age. She has experienced the rawness of human emotion and brings to her writing that of a fellow struggler, yet with hope, faith, and love.

In reading the rough draft of <u>Gutsy Little Flowers</u>, I again went to my favorite chair and read it from cover to cover. As I turned the last page, I thought to myself, "Cathy has done it again!"

She has written her story in such a way that I connected . . . deeply connected with her story, with myself, with the central message of hope and strength in tough times, and I experienced God's presence.

As a pastor I wish I could make this required reading for my congregation because it will bring sunshine to those in darkness, hope to those who feel hopeless, and courage to those who are weak and in despair. Most of all, it will be an instrument for understanding more about the character and love of God and how that love sustains us in and through the seasons of life.

So. . . I encourage you to go to your favorite reading place, grab a cup of coffee, put your feet up and begin a journey with Cathy Lee Phillips . . . with yourself. Her words will feel like a pair of old, comfortable shoes. We will feel again what we already know but somehow have forgotten, and we will be strengthened to walk a little taller, stand a little sturdier and move forward with greater hope – and "guts" – on this road called life.

D. B. Shelnutt, Jr.
Johns Creek United Methodist Church
Duluth, Georgia

Acknowledgements

What do you say when you have realized a long-held dream?

Writing has been my dream for as long as I can recall. But, as so often happens, my dream took a back seat as *LIFE* took priority. Each day, it seemed, demanded far more than I could accomplish (still true!). There simply was no time to write, although my dream of writing remained very much alive.

One day, though, I was hit hard with the brevity of life. About the same time a very wise lady took me aside and bluntly said, "Cathy, I have a word for you. You are meant to write. You have so many stories and if you do not tell them, they will never be told. And I, for one, am going to be upset if I do not get to hear them."

She smiled and walked away, leaving me stunned and speechless, and thankful . . . because she was right. You had better believe that I rushed home that night and started writing -- and I haven't stopped since. I do have stories to tell, I have discovered. I see them everywhere, in all sorts of people, places and experiences. And, though I struggle over each and every word, I do want to tell stories that will, hopefully, lead each of us a little closer to God.

I can honestly say that I never expected the overwhelming reaction I received to <u>Silver in the Slop</u>. "My little pig book," as I often call it, has obviously touched many of you. You have honored me with your cards, letters, e-mails, calls, and words of support. You have also honored me with many invitations to meet and share with you through retreats, speaking, and singing engagements. I have had a great time!

But I am sincere in asking that you thank God – not me – if these words have cheered, comforted, or challenged you. To be honest, writing is hard work for me and I have often been tempted to simply walk away from my computer . . . but God draws me back. This is what I am meant to do. I know that very clearly now. I know that from your reaction to <u>Silver in the Slop</u>. I also know it by the way I am continually drawn back to the computer when I honestly feel that I cannot write another word.

So, what do you say when you have realized a long-held dream?

I have to say "thank you" to God. I have to say "thank you" to the people who are important in my life. And I have to say "thank you" to the many of you who have read my books and articles, purchased books, and extended invitations to be a part of your meetings, retreats, and events. Bless you all!

I am so grateful to my very special friend, Dr. D. B. Shelnutt, who still allows me to call him Dee despite all his degrees and honors. You have truly honored me by taking the time to write the foreword to this book.

To Deborah – you are an A+ friend, sister, and chauffer (on two-way streets). You are also the best Project Manager that Patchwork Press, Ltd. could possibly have. Nurse Helga lives!

To Jim – I consider you my manager, my advisor, but my friend first and foremost.

To all the Huyckes (plus Bob Bob and Dell) – the word is "family." Enough said!

To Mary – Nobody knows the trouble we've seen. But no group of letters (DSREVSPR) could take away our faith or our laughter, even while sitting in the hot seats. Thanks for keeping me from going (coco) nuts!

To the Branhams – For the laughs, the long conversations, and the times we spend together – I love you all, sis!

To Caroline – You are the Queen of proofreading, a terrific Webmaster, and a friend who is usually there when I'm in a "Corner."

To Virginia – Thanks for reappearing just when I needed another surrogate mom, good friend, public relations manager, and a Vice President of Sales all rolled up in one incredible person.

To Eric – You've given me the gift of a home base, "deep" conversations, laughter, support, and true flexibility. You are the best.

To Gwen – Keep singing, girl! Thanks for a growing friendship.

To Lauren – the friendship goes on and we will, no doubt cry and laugh together for years to come. I am thankful for you as well as the rest of the Biggs family. It is wonderful that you have been "transplanted" to JCUMC. Make Dee behave!

To Betty W. – You have no idea how wonderful it is to be checked on every few days. Are you worried that I might get into trouble? You're a terrific mom and one tough chick.

To Norma, Sybil, Toni, and Margaret – I am blessed with a bunch of terrific moms. Thank you for never once placing me on restriction. But, where is my allowance?

To Don and Betty – I can't imagine life without you. You have always been there and I love you for that. Got any gossip?

To Janice – Regarding Scarritt, Rock Springs Apartments, White Somersets, Grace, etc. -- Do you have a problem with originality? At least you are one of a kind when it comes to friends. Hi John!

To Neil – Thank you for challenging me to write outside the box. There will be more to come.

To Marty – Have I told you that I consider you an adopted brother? An older brother, of course. Connie and Margaret have been family for a long time. Just don't make me responsible for Corey's and Ashley's college tuition.

To Joe – No words can do you justice – and that is an understatement. But I'm glad you, Angel, and Ryan are part of the family. (Well, at least the last two, anyway).

To Phyllis – 1974? Boy, that seems like so long ago. I'm ready for Alaska, the sequel.

My sincere appreciation also goes to the many bookstore managers who have taken a chance on <u>Silver in the Slop</u> and to the many who purchased and read my little pig book.

To those who have allowed your stories to be included in the pages of this book, you have my gratitude.

A special word of thanks goes to the Ladies and Gentlemen of the Ritz Carlton, Amelia Island, who welcome me back each year with pampering and pink roses.

And to Jerry – You are celebrating with me, aren't you? Perfect love transcends time and space.

As before, to all those mentioned above, the *SECOND* book is finished. Let's party!

Cathy Lee Phillips
Canton, Georgia
October 2001

Winter in my soul.

Will spring ever come again?

Jonquils bloom in snow.

Gutsy Little Flowers

*H*ave you seen the jonquils? They are making their appearances in yards and fields all around us. Gutsy little flowers, they are!

While winter still holds us in its icy grip, these yellow messengers of spring listen to the Voice of Creation that says, "It's time. You can bloom now."

Beneath the frozen ground the sleeping bulb stirs, bursts open, and a tiny green shoot fights its way toward the surface of the cold earth. Even while tree limbs fall from the weight of winter ice, the green shoot pushes through the hard soil and a tiny yellow bud begins to form. Barely noticeable at first, the bloom opens slowly until a brilliant golden flower appears, standing bravely against the frigid temperatures and the briskly blowing wind. Even as the snow falls, the jonquil grows. This ordinary little flower stands as a precious reminder of spring amid a world weary of the gloom of winter.

Winter has its place, of course. Winter is a warm sweater, a cup of hot chocolate, a crackling fireplace, the joy of Christmas, and the dawn of a New Year. Winter in Georgia is the occasional snow and ice that, for a day or so, slows us down and provides moments of quiet solitude and reflection. But, soon enough, the bleak, frosty days of winter create within us a longing for the warmth of sunshine on our faces and a new season of life.

Then, just when we need them most, God sends the jonquils, bright and yellow, standing in brave contrast to the gray days of winter. The jonquils – simple yet beautiful reminders that spring is coming to take its place in the cycle of creation.

The jonquils, though, are not alone in their resurrection celebration. You see, a winter of doubt and darkness gripped the hearts of many standing before a cross on an agonizing day thousands of years ago.

But, even that bleak day on a hill called Golgotha could not stop the Voice of the Creator who, just three days later said, "It's time. You can bloom now." And just when it seemed that this bleak winter of grief and anguish would last forever, Jesus Christ stirred and inhaled deeply the breath of life even in the darkness of a musty tomb. And when no one was looking, He burst forth in a miracle of resurrection that forever changed a world starved for new life. Leaving behind the darkness, our Savior shook off the bonds of death and revealed that new life was possible.

The jonquils know the story because each year they experience new life themselves. They are buried and forgotten for a time until the bulb opens, grows toward the light, and reminds us that new life is possible.

But the jonquils are not alone. We, too, can hear the same Voice of Creation that says, "It's time. You can bloom now."

And heeding the stirring deep within our own hearts, we understand that the time has come to shake off the cold of winter within us that holds past mistakes, former habits, old fears and anxieties. Then, with our eyes trained upward, we may grow from the green shoot to a small bud and, finally, a golden blossom that bears witness to the precious gift of new life amid a world weary of the dreariness of winter.

I have been a jonquil before. Haven't you? There have been times in my life when it seemed winter would last forever – times of adversity and hurt, times of loss and grief, times of confusion and distress. You, too, have experienced these days, no doubt.

But consider this. Though we may not understand, we are evolving even in our winter moments. Every hurt challenges us to turn to God as the Great Physician. Every loss reminds us that Christ promised that we who mourn shall be comforted. Every period of confusion teaches us to turn to God for the peace that passes all understanding. Every dark day dares us to wait confidently for the warmth of the sun that, in the fullness of time, will shine again.

And when the time is right for each of us, we will hear the Voice of Creation say, "It's time. You can bloom now!"

Then, just like the gusty little flowers, we overcome. Even when the odds are against us and the days are cold and long, we fight to take our place in the world, stronger and more beautiful because we *have overcome*. With the jonquils, we remind the world that the winters we encounter are not eternal. Pain and tears do not last forever. Not even death itself has the final answer. We, too, give witness to resurrection, to new life, and to the everlasting love of God.

Have you seen the jonquils? They have begun their dance of new life.

They are inviting you to join the celebration.

For, lo, the winter is past,
the rain is over and gone;
the flowers appear on the earth;
the time of the singing of birds is come,
and the voice of the turtle dove
is heard in our land.

Song of Solomon 2:11-12

I Still Love You, Norman Rockwell!

Overcoming the less-than-perfect Christmas

Wrapped in a pale blue quilted robe and white knee socks, I stretched my feet toward the warmth of the fire. The temperature outside hovered around 10 degrees that frigid Christmas night and the power of our wood heater was not sufficient to warm the whole house. So, seeking warmth, all others took to their beds in various places throughout the cold house. I sat alone by the wood heater with the Christmas tree as my sole companion.

Staring at the tree I decided that it was most likely the ugliest Christmas tree in all of Georgia, yea verily, most likely in all of the United States.

It barely seemed a tree at all. It was more an odd collection of skinny, scraggly branches joined at a knotty trunk. A cedar from the woods near the pond on Posey Road, our tree-wanna-be in no way resembled the perfect trees found in Norman Rockwell's celebrated paintings.

How I longed for a Norman Rockwell tree to grace our living room! Instead, I sat beside this unshapely, uneven, and seriously ugly bundle of branches and bald spots. Furthermore, instead of the magnificent decorations worthy of a Norman

Rockwell tree, this pitiful object was adorned only with a few old glass balls, a box of cheap silver icicles, and a string of eight Christmas lights.

That string of lights had been a fixture in our house for years. It consisted of one empty socket that no longer worked, two red lights, one blue light, one green light, and three orange lights. While those seven lights did their very best, they were no match for this overpowering mass of skinny, scraggly branches. In short, there was far more tree than light. Seven lights – and three of them orange. What did orange lights have to do with Christmas anyway? Norman Rockwell would certainly never place ugly orange lights on his Christmas trees. No, his paintings were filled with hundreds of tiny picturesque white bulbs pointing the way to a beautiful white angel serenely crowning his perfectly-shaped Christmas tree. Of course, there was no angel on our tree -- only a cardboard star covered with aluminum foil.

I hated that star. I hated that tree. And I especially hated those three orange lights. I suddenly grew very weary of all the fuss and frustration of Christmas.

The only thing I really enjoyed was the pity party I experienced that Christmas night that fixed my mind, at least for a while, on those three orange lights instead of the truth of Christmas. Pulling the blue robe closer, my anger softened as I remembered another Christmas night when the world was weary and cynical, but rejoiced when a light shone in the heavens proclaiming the miraculous birth of a baby in a manger.

And though that miracle happened thousands of years before, I was faced with a choice that lonely Christmas night. I could be consumed by my resentment of Norman Rockwell and three orange lights and remain a weary, pitiful soul.

Or, I could change my attitude and, even in a blue quilted robe seated next to a wood heater and the ugliest Christmas tree in all of Georgia, yea verily, most likely all of the United States, I could celebrate the miracle of that first Christmas night.

I made my decision.

The ugliest tree in Georgia would not take away the joy of Christmas for me. A Norman Rockwell painting would not define Christmas for me. And three orange lights would not keep me from finding what I needed most that night – the true light of the world shining through the anger in my heart.

Jesus was born anew in my heart that night and I almost missed the moment because of loneliness, anger, Norman Rockwell, one seriously ugly tree, and three orange Christmas lights.

> *"I am the light of the world;*
> *he that followeth me shall not walk in darkness,*
> *but shall have the light of life."*
> *(John 8:12)*

I have a hope for you for all the Christmases to come. It doesn't consist of Norman Rockwell paintings and orange Christmas lights. I simply hope that, like me, you may look past the frustrations of a less-than-perfect holiday and meet anew the true light of heaven, the baby born to become the Savior of the world.

*Now when Jesus was born
in Bethlehem in Judea, behold,
there came wise men from the east
to Jerusalem, saying,
"Where is he that is born
King of the Jews?
for we have seen his star in the east,
and are come to worship him."*

Matthew 2:1-2

New Year Meditation

*T*he ball dropped, the confetti fell, and on a very special January 1, the year 2000 began. To the surprise of some, the world kept spinning. No millennium bug ate my computer nor, to my knowledge, did aliens from unknown galaxies descend to rule the earth. In fact, the moment came and went and life continued pretty much as usual. It is just that it feels so strange to say "the year 2000-something" instead of "19-something."

I think I was probably in the third grade when I first calculated the age I would be when the year 2000 arrived. Forty-three! And it seemed soooo old! I wondered what I would be doing when that magical date was a reality. I suppose I envisioned a happy marriage, a well-to-do, loving husband (okay, picture Mel Gibson), a lavish house (with Jacuzzi), 2.5 perfect children, an exciting career – you know, the typical things.

Some things have materialized, but others will never happen. But I have seen and done and experienced more than my child's mind ever dared to imagine. My highs have been moments of ecstasy as I praised God for His greatness. But there have also been those inevitable lows, some of which I felt would surely destroy my faith, my hope, even me.

9

But they didn't!

The year 2000 and then 2001 arrived and I am still here. And now forty-three seems soooo young! Without a doubt, each new year will hold its typical share of highs and lows for all of us. While I certainly do not know what each day will bring, I do know who will face each day with me.

For I am convinced that nothing shall separate me – shall separate us – from God. These familiar words from the eighth chapter of Romans remind us that *"neither death, nor life, nor angels, nor principalities, nor powers, nor things present, nor things to come, nor height, nor depth, nor any other creature, shall be able to separate us from the love of God, which is in Christ Jesus our Lord."* We can add our own fears and worries to this list – neither the uncertainty of a new year, nor the highest highs, nor the lowest lows, will be able to separate us from the love of God.

Nothing that happens today, tomorrow, for the remainder of this century, or for eternity, will separate us from God. Rest securely in this promise and, with it guiding your every step, walk confidently into the future with your head held high and your hand resting safely in the loving grip of your Father.

> *What shall we say then to these things?*
> *If God be for us,*
> *who can be against us?*
>
> *Romans 8:31*

Go Ahead – Share Your Basket

*T*hough a touch of winter chill was in the air, the Easter morning held a promise of warmth that would come with the rising sun.

Across the room Raylinda Dupree, the scourge of my childhood, slept soundly. My cousin twice-removed on my Mama's side, Raylinda was the meanest person I knew. In fact, she was the meanest person most people knew. She lived with us after her parents divorced and quickly made an impression on the other residents of Posey Road. Within days of her arrival she had been awarded various nicknames including, but not limited to, "Satan's Star Student." While I know God loves us all, Raylinda certainly did put her best efforts into earning her reputation.

Snoring loudly, Raylinda stirred only when Mama mentioned two words – Easter Baskets! Racing to the dining room table, Raylinda and I found two wicker baskets crammed with all the items essential to the Posey Road Easter Basket. Atop green plastic grass sat colorful luscious eggs, tangy jellybeans, tiny football-shaped chocolate wrapped in pastel foil, yellow marshmallow chicks, and a vast collection of speckled malted milk eggs. Four wrapped eggs with various fruit fillings

11

were placed strategically at north, sound, east, and west within the basket. A hollow bunny inside a colorful box rested amid the green grass. And, of course, the traditional focal point of the basket was a large coconut egg covered in chocolate with a candy flower adorning the top.

As I examined my basket, I realized that Raylinda had disappeared. While I considered her absence an Easter blessing, Mama was frustrated. It was going to be a busy day beginning with the annual Sunrise Service at 6:30 a.m. Because Mama played the piano, we could not be late for church. Breakfast and Sunday School would follow the Sunrise Service. At 11:00 a.m. our little church would fill with people dressed in their Easter best, many of whom we had not seen since Christmas. People would happily greet one another and a festive spirit would fill the air. We would sing my favorite Easter hymn, *"Up from the grave He arose with a mighty triumph o'er his foes"* with a force that shook the walls in celebration.

Raylinda, of course, sang her own version: *"Up from the grave He arose with a trumpet sticking in His nose."* She sang loudly and off-key while many stared and frowned at "Satan's Star Student."

After church, we hurried home and waited for extended family and friends to arrive for a huge Easter dinner. Mama baked ham and everyone brought food to share. The general idea was to eat until you could barely move.

There was an unspoken rule that the ladies would each try to outdo the other when it came to dessert. There was a 5-layer strawberry cake with fresh strawberries decorating the top. An Italian Cream Cake was Aunt Zelma's annual contribution. There was always a huge banana pudding (Oh Lord, I hate bananas!) Then, of course, there were several new recipes straight from the pages of the latest Good Housekeeping or Southern Living Magazines. While some adults did indulge in these exquisite homemade offerings, many simply wanted a couple of malted eggs to top off their ham and potato salad.

Those decisions, of course, only irritated the bakers of the Good Housekeeping and Southern Living fancy desserts.

This was the moment each child brought his or her Easter Basket to show and share. The only object not subject to sharing, said Mama, was our large coconut egg. It was safely tucked away in the back of the refrigerator. Everything else was fair game and communal property. In other words, it was open season on Easter Baskets.

About this time I finally understood the reason for Raylinda's strange disappearance earlier that morning. As she begrudgingly shared her basket, it swiftly passed from one person to the next. No one partook of any item in Raylinda's basket. When I looked closely, I instantly discovered the reason. It was clearly evident that someone had taken a bite out of every piece of candy in the basket. Each tiny egg had been unwrapped and nibbled. Teeth marks adorned every jellybean and malted milk piece. The hollow chocolate bunny rattled inside his box because someone had chewed away his ears. And every innocent little marshmallow chick was headless!

Adults were appalled. Other kids were angry. Granny gasped and held her chest. Aunt Zelma became woozy with the vapors.

The basket was a sacrilege. Blasphemy on Easter Sunday! Who would perform such a cruel, selfish act?

The answer was obvious to me. To keep from sharing, Satan's Star Student had taken a bite out of every object in her basket. She was stingy. She was mean. And she had just demonstrated that truth to everyone present.

Her shameful behavior never changed. Not only did Raylinda succeed in protecting her basket that particular Easter, she continued to do so each year. No one wanted to partake of the damaged goods in her basket so she succeeded in keeping all candy to herself. Raylinda easily kept her well-earned reputation of being the meanest, greediest person I knew.

Raylinda's greed did not stop Easter, of course. It simply proved that all humans are flawed in one way or another – some perhaps more than others! Years later, I realize that Raylinda, in her selfishness, demonstrated one of the real truths of the season.

Easter is not about greed. It has nothing to do with selfishness.

Easter has everything to do with love and sharing. It celebrates a wondrous moment when, to a flawed world, God gave His very best in the form of a child in a manger. God gave this gift to each of us, fully and freely, holding nothing back.

No, Easter is not about greed. Therefore, we should never hesitate to share the Good News of Easter with everyone.

There are many things I will never understand. But this I do know – God gave His best to us. And God expects the best from us.

So, I suppose, it is possible to learn a positive lesson even from Raylinda Dupree, the scourge of my childhood and "Satan's Star Student." Thank God for the blessing of Jesus Christ and the priceless gift of eternal life. Then, in a spirit of true gratitude, praise God by joyfully and unselfishly sharing your basket!

For God so loved the world
that He gave His only begotten Son
that whosoever believeth in Him
should not perish
but have everlasting life.

John 3:16

Attack of the Killer Flypaper

Overcoming Our Imagined Fears

*I*t was a big hair day. I made that decision on a whim, little knowing the events it would set into motion. This was a few years ago when "big" hair was in style and I had just received a new perm in my auburn (absolutely no gray, of course!) locks. Because my curls were shoulder length, I occasionally used a variety of accessories to corral my hair into a sleek ponytail or other various styles. However, on this particular day I opted for the tousled, carefree, big-hair look – a decision I would live to regret. I finished the style with half a bottle of mega spritz, a glue-like spray that provided my big hair the power to withstand a hurricane.

My husband and I were in a hurry that morning. Jerry was flying to Colorado Springs for a convention of the United Methodist Association of Church Business Administrators. I would fight the Atlanta traffic going toward the airport, drop Jerry off in time to catch his flight, and then fight more traffic to reach my office on the other side of Atlanta.

My schedule that day was quite full, including a lunch appointment and several afternoon meetings. Leaving my office that afternoon, I fought more traffic, ran a gazillion errands, met friends for dinner, and returned home well after 11:00 that dark night.

Though I was completely exhausted, I was proud that my big hair still looked fresh thanks to its three-inch glaze of mega-spritz.

Crawling into bed that night, I was almost asleep when I realized I had forgotten one very important task. Rhett and Ashley were waiting on their dinner! Rhett and Ashley were two beautiful cocker spaniels – one black and one blonde – who did not want to suffer hunger pangs all night long. Feeding them was normally Jerry's job but he had safely arrived in Colorado and had no intention of flying home to feed two cocker spaniels, no matter how special they were.

"Those two dogs will surely live until morning," I rationalized, "and they could actually stand to lose a pound or two." I snuggled further under the cover and punched the pillow into a comfortable position.

I tried to sleep but the faces of those two lovable old dogs appeared each time I closed my eyes. I was warm and comfortable and did not want to crawl out of bed. But there was a bigger issue at stake.

I, Cathy Lee Phillips, am afraid of the dark. I grew up where there was talk of boogers and monsters and haints and such – a virtual smorgasbord of creatures just waiting to grab and torment me in the night. *(A word of explanation may be necessary for the Yankees or the very young among us – "haint" is an old southern word meaning anything scary, frightening, or just generally creepy).* Though talk of these creatures took place during my childhood, I remained convinced that boogers and monsters and haints still awaited me in the dark.

So, while I was warm and comfortable in bed that night, I primarily did not want to face the terrors of the dark. But, my love for these old dogs prevailed and I reluctantly climbed out of bed, pulled a purple chenille robe over my still perfect big hair and slipped my feet inside my Nikes.

16

What a picture I was that midnight – a weirdly dressed, scared-of-the-dark, big haired preacher's wife facing boogers and monsters and haints to undertake a mission of mercy for two beloved cocker spaniels.

Rhett and Ashley lived in a "doggie condo" behind our parsonage. Inside their fence was a shed that housed them, a riding mower, assorted junk, and an ample supply of Wal-Mart Old Roy dog food. It also housed an abundance of flies, quite possibly attracted to the halo of mega-spritz encircling our house.

What I did not know, and what Jerry failed to tell me before he boarded his flight that morning, was that the shed also housed something else that dark night. You see, my dear husband decided to tackle the problem of those pesky flies with an age-old remedy – flypaper. About two inches wide, the flypaper came in little canisters that hooked to the roof of the building and hung approximately three feet from the ceiling. The desired effect, of course, was that flies and mosquitoes would innocently crash into this sticky substance where they would remain until their bodies were lifeless.

Jerry, I must say, was very efficient when it came to dealing with annoying flying creatures and was not content to simply suspend one or two strips of flypaper. No! He virtually covered the ceiling of that little shed with a truckload of sticky strips hanging from the ceiling . . . just waiting for his mega-spritzed, big-haired wife . . . who also had a fear of the dark and its imagined collection of boogers, monsters, and haints.

"Oh, didn't I tell you about the flypaper?" Jerry innocently asked later.

You see this coming, right? As I bent down to open the plastic container of Wal-Mart Old Roy dog food, I luckily avoided the flypaper. But as I stood up straight (all 5 feet, 0 inches of me), my big hair felt a tug. My head was pulled backwards and I was suddenly encased in something unknown and very sinister. In the eerie darkness I did not realize that it was me, not the mosquitoes, that the flypaper had captured so skillfully.

Sections of flypaper seized my big hair while others slapped at my face. The harder I fought, the harder my unknown enemy fought back. The flypaper seized my hair and the fuzzy material of my chenille robe. It stuck to me as I flailed my arms and bravely battled the boogers and monsters and haints I envisioned. My heart pounded as I shrieked and, with great effort, finally broke free from the invisible enemy tormenting me. I raced toward the safety of the parsonage where I slammed, bolted the door, and tried to breath normally again. Running to the bathroom, I faced my reflection in the large mirror. It was not a pretty sight. Staring back at me was a terrorized preacher's wife complete with Tammy Faye mascara running from my panic-stricken eyes while my big hair looked as though it had been brushed in a blender and dipped in mega-spritz and flypaper.

It was well past 3:00 a.m. before my heart stopped pounding and the final remnants of flypaper were pulled from my big hair.

I did not have a happy attitude.

In fact, I was still scared. Circumstances had converged that night to exploit my fears and make me just plain mad.

After a few hours of restless sleep, the alarm sounded and woke me in time to get dressed and fight the Atlanta traffic for another day. I washed my hair and pulled it back into a sleek ponytail that hid most of the bald spots caused by extracting the cursed flypaper. Before leaving for work, in the fullness of daylight, I returned to the doggie condo and fed Rhett and Ashley a double helping of Wal-Mart Old Roy dog food.

While I have never looked a roll of flypaper in the face again, I still have days when terror and darkness grip my heart. There is much to fear in our imperfect world. When my fears, real or imagined, threaten to overtake me, I hold tightly to comforting words from Romans 8:15 – *"For ye have not received the spirit of bondage to fear; but ye have received the Spirit of adoption, whereby we cry, Abba, Father."*

Tomorrow beckons – a new day in which anything can happen. Many days will be joyous, of course. But there will also be days we feel the presence of boogers and monsters and haints triggering fear and anxiety.

My advice?

Boldly face those days with your hair small, your faith big, and walk confidently with a loving God who understands your anxiety and gently whispers, "Fear not!"

*The Lord is my light
and my salvation;
whom shall I fear?
The Lord is the strength of my life;
of whom shall I be afraid?*

Psalm 27:1

19

Cathy Lee Phillips

Safely Resting
In Her Father's Arms

Overcoming the Terror of Losing a Loved One

*T*hough it has been more than twelve years, I can still see their faces clearly.

The father. Each day he occupied the same chair – an ugly pale green vinyl creation with wooden legs and a straight back. The chair was situated in the back right corner of the waiting room, in a dimly lit area far from the door. I think he chose that spot purposefully – the shadows allowed his daughter to sleep and obscured his tears that flowed so freely. Men aren't supposed to cry, some say. But from my chair across the aisle, I could see his pain. He wept silently, large tears filling his sad brown eyes before spilling quietly down his cheeks.

The child. I never saw her eyes. They were closed each day in a peaceful sleep as she safely rested in her father's arms. Two years old, maybe three, she was wrapped tightly each day in the same pale pink fuzzy blanket. The only visible part of her body was a delicate face that peeked through the warmth of the blanket. Her face was framed with a ruffled white cap she wore daily to hide the hair that was no longer there. She displayed the unmistakable color of the cancer that weakened her tiny body and brought the tears to her father's eyes. So still, so silent, the little girl never moved, never woke, never cried. There was no need for her to cry – her father's tears spoke more than enough for both of them.

The place. A crowded and depressing waiting room at Atlanta's Emory University Hospital. Every patient shared two things – cancer and waiting his or her turn at receiving the radiation designed to destroy the terrifying disease. I was there each day with my mother. She had cancer. It was a secondary problem related to another illness she had endured for many years. Surgery had removed her tumor, but five weeks of radiation was a necessary step to, hopefully, prevent the return of the cancer. While I waited for my mother to receive her treatment, I could not help but observe the anguished father who held his fragile little girl in a loving embrace.

It was a heartbreaking scene. I never knew the type of cancer that assaulted the young child's body. I did not know any of the circumstances surrounding her life. How long had she been ill? What was her name? Had she known happy, laughter-filled days before the disease struck? And why was her father the only one to bring her for treatment? Was her mother working? Dead? Too grief-stricken herself to come to the hospital? Or maybe this marriage did not survive the pressure and pain of a child's prolonged illness. Many do not.

As I wondered about the child, I agonized with the father. I never spoke to him. His need for privacy was apparent; his heartache more than obvious. His tears were so abundant it seemed that surely they would carve permanent furrows down the front of his face.

How he loved that child! She was so ill that she might have been a burden to some. She was so silent she could not talk or play or laugh with her father, so weak she was unable to throw her arms around him in a massive bear hug. While her body battled the cancer, she was too weak for anything but sleep. So she lay in his arms, still and quiet, completely incapable of doing anything to *earn* his love.

But she did not have to do anything to earn his love.

Simply by *being* she was loved. Love was evident as the man wept and held her with gentle strength in his loving arms. Love was evident in the pale pink blanket and the ruffled cap covering her tiny bald head. Love was so evident that I knew, without having to ask, that this father would gladly sacrifice his life for his child. Though this grim waiting room was saturated with dread and despair, it could not drive out a father's obvious and immeasurable love.

Despite her illness, I realized how blessed this child was. To receive a love so great is a gift beyond measure.

"But I have that!" I quickly remembered.

Deep inside I am a tiny child who lacks the strength to do all I need to do. I am a tiny child with an imperfect body that causes me pain and frustration. I am a tiny child who wants to be wrapped in a blanket of love and held until all my hurts go away. I am a tiny child who can never do enough to *earn* the love of my Heavenly Father.

But I do not have to earn his love. Simply by being a child of His, I am loved. God surrounds me with a love so great that He sacrificed a life for mine – the life of *His* only child.

Even now, when I am tired or sick or weary, my Father carries me in arms so powerful they created an entire universe; arms so gentle they tenderly cradle my head while He wipes away all tears from my eyes; arms so strong that they never tire of holding me so that I may sleep peacefully.

It has been more than twelve years and I can still see the faces of the father and his daughter. I do not know what happened to this tiny child and, from time to time, I wonder about her. Is she running and playing and laughing with friends? Is she opening gifts on Christmas and receiving a surprise birthday party this year? Has she held hands with her boyfriend as they shared an awkward first kiss? Does she talk on the phone until late at night and share secrets with a best friend? Is her father watching proudly from the sidelines as she shoots a basketball or hits a softball down the left field line?

Or does she, instead, sit in the strong lap of Jesus Christ as she giggles and hugs His neck? Does she tug on Moses' beard or twirl her own long, golden locks of hair? Does she walk the streets amid the beauty of paradise? Does she play on the shore of a heavenly sea, secure in the knowledge that, one day, she will be united with her earthly father?

I do not know. I probably will never know.

But, I am certain of one thing. Wherever she is – in this world or the next – tonight this child will again safely rest in the arms of a loving Father.

> *He shall feed His flock like a shepherd:*
> *He shall gather the lambs*
> *with his arm,*
> *and carry them in His bosom,*
> *and shall gently lead those*
> *that are with young.*
>
> *Isaiah 40:11*

The Mammogram

Overcoming Fear of the "C" Word

Dedicated to Betty Wallace,
my "Mom" and wonderful friend
who has faced her own battle with breast cancer with
grace, dignity, courage, humor and an unwavering faith.
You inspire me – I love you!

*T*he call came at work on a Thursday afternoon. It was the kind of call you never want to receive – the call that tells you something is wrong. This time it was a spot on a mammogram I had just days before.

"Now, don't panic," the doctor stressed.

I hate when someone tells me that. My brain translates that phrase into: *If there ever was a time to panic, cry, crawl in a corner, suck your thumb, wet your pants, and otherwise go crazy, the time is now.* As the doctor continued, I seriously considered doing all of the above – and I was at the office! I had my funeral plans complete before the call ended. After all, this was not a tonsillectomy or a knee repair. In the instant of a ringing phone, I was looking squarely into the face of the "C" word.

"This is probably just a benign mass," the very calm doctor continued. "It is just that we have no point of comparison because this is your baseline mammogram. The mass could have been there for 20 years. We just have no way of knowing."

I had just turned 40 – more good news – and being a responsible "over-the-hiller" I followed the recommendation of the medical community and scheduled my first mammogram. That was bad enough! My technician, Gia, did everything she could to make me comfortable. But, ladies, let's be realistic. There is simply no way to enjoy being exposed from the waist up while leaning your privates into a modern-day machine of torture designed to squeeze, squish and scrunch certain beloved body parts into unnatural, non-God-intended positions. But there I was – standing practically naked and vulnerable before this massive monster as Gia took her place behind a protective shield.

"Take a deep breath and hold it," she instructed, fully clothed, standing a safe distance from the radiation making its way into my chest. "And don't move!"

Yea, right! Even if I had tried to run, part of me would have forever remained squeezed beyond recognition, pinned beneath the layers of this state-of-the-art instrument of agony.

If that experience were not horrible enough, my knees were suddenly turning to rubber as I listened to my doctor explain that the evil machine had found something "abnormal."

I wanted my mama.

I wanted anybody's mama.

But, no. I was at work with three very typical (clueless?) men who were wondering why a mere telephone call had reduced me to tears. And being very typical men, the best advice they could muster was, "Try not to worry."

Wow. And it took the collective wisdom of all three men to produce that pearl of wisdom.

My doctor arranged a second mammogram plus an ultrasound for the following morning. Perhaps a different view of the area would provide further detail. Or if the mass was visible via ultrasound, it meant the spot was probably just a fluid-filled cyst.

The next day, though, the ultrasound showed nothing. That meant the suspicious area was definitely a solid mass. That also meant I had to endure a "compression" mammogram, an agonizing procedure conceived, no doubt, from the depraved mind of a male undeniably plagued by a deep-seated hatred of the female of the species.

"Compression" was an interesting experience (sarcasm, get it?). For approximately 20 minutes a complete stranger placed my aforementioned body part between two large metal plates. They clamped down upon me with the weight of an 18-wheeler hauling hogs and squeezed until I thought the mass – along with my chest – would surely explode. Once that point was reached, the technician gave the machine two more twists until I bit my lip and saw stars dancing before my eyes. I was compressed to practically nothing. In fact, an A-cup would have laughed in my face!

My doctor called again the following day. The suspicious area was still present and, even after my chest being compressed beyond anything recognizable, the medical experts could not determine the origin of the mass. My anxiety filled me with a cold sweat as I realized the horrifying fact that I had a lump in my breast that could very well be cancerous. The doctor then presented me with two options: (A) wait for six months and see if the mass grew or (B) undergo surgery to have the mass removed and biopsied.

I feel it necessary to pause momentarily and attempt to explain my severe, out-of-control, dreadful, and terrifying fear of doctors, nurses, tests, and generally anything medical. My panic is real. I have been intimately acquainted with serious illness since I was five years old. My mother saw a doctor and was told she had a terminal disease. My husband saw a doctor and was told he needed a heart transplant. Therefore, reason tells me that if I have a headache, I obviously have a brain tumor. If my stomach is queasy, I obviously have stomach cancer. And on it goes . . . This is an awful phobia and a source of great dread and frustration in my life.

While I am afraid of anything medical, surgery definitely tops the list. Yet as afraid as I am of surgery, I have had surgery six (six!) times. Yep, three knee operations, carpal tunnel surgery on each hand, and one tonsillectomy at age twenty-six. The tonsillectomy was, by far, the most painful and the most humiliating.

It is a distressing feeling to lie on a table in a cold operating room knowing that you are about to be placed in some out-of-it zone while strangers cut, plunder and, quite possibly, laugh, at your privates. In addition, the feeling of being out of control is terrifying beyond description. In short, I would do anything to avoid having surgery . . . almost. The idea of allowing a possibly cancerous mass to grow inside me for six months was a stupid option and one I had no intention of following. Despite my terror, I opted for surgery to remove the suspicious mass.

My nerves were shot and the date for surgery had not even been scheduled.

I spoke with several individuals who explained the "wire localization" procedure I would undergo. The practice involved another trip to the now-familiar machine of torture where I would, once again, be compressed so that the exact location of the evil mass could be determined. Technicians would use a graph to plot its location and then spear it – right down the middle – with a long wire. This would show the surgeon where to cut and, therefore, keep him from digging for buried treasure without benefit of a map.

Groovy.

The wire localization could be tricky as two technicians tried to align and pierce the mass according to a graph. They spoke to each other in numbers – B2, C4, F7 – in what sounded like Hell's version of Bingo. When they felt reasonably sure they had located the area, the wire was inserted. OUCH! And, as my luck goes, they did not "spear" the mass on the first try.

The procedure was repeated, successfully on the second try. The wire properly intersected the growth and, as a final touch, a small metal ball resembling something found on a fishing line was twisted onto the end of the wire to keep it from sinking further into me and away from the growth. Thus, I was rolled into surgery feeling very much like a bizarre prop for Orlando Wilson's Fishing Show. I stared at the wire and the metal ball that drifted in rhythm with the gurney as I was rolled, exposed and terrified, toward the Operating Room.

My friends, Jennifer and Mimi, accompanied me to the "unveiling and slicing." God has blessed me with many good friends, and these are two of the best! Indeed, they had to be good friends in order to accompany me to the place of my greatest fear. They remained with me during the pre-op procedure as doctors waited on the "joy juice" they placed into my veins to calm my nerves. They waited . . . and waited . . . but even a second dose of "joy juice" did not calm me. My heart raced faster than the Space Shuttle darting toward the heavens. Before I arrived at the hospital, I had experienced an "un-Cathy-like" calmness that, by now, was a distant memory. Once the pre-op procedure began, however, Jennifer and Mimi watched me turn into a thumb-sucking mass of quivering nerves. But, bless them, they know my phobia and love me anyway. Either that or they simply came along to watch the show! My friends waved at me from the hallway as I was rolled – cold, bare-chested, and ready to cry -- to the operating room.

Things moved quickly once I arrived in the operating room. A variety of people I had never met walked about performing their jobs very efficiently while I was placed on the operating table. This collection of strangers seemed not to care that I was naked from the waist up. Still, I couldn't help but wonder if they would talk about me once I entered la-la land.

"Just talk and tell me what you are doing," I pleaded as a blood pressure cuff, heart monitor, and other items were attached to me. I tried to explain my terror and the fact that their talking to me eased my tension.

My surgeon finally entered the room and said, "Cathy, how are you doing?"

I will not even begin to describe the response I wanted to give. Biting back the colorful words I was thinking, I simply responded, "I'm just fine."

"We are going to put you to sleep now and everything will be over when you wake up."

I did not want to be put to sleep. But I certainly did not want to stay awake for this either. And I had to wonder whether everything would really be over or was this procedure just the beginning of a battle with breast cancer. These pleasant thoughts crowded my mind as I fought momentary dizziness before entering the world of the unconscious.

"Cathy?"

I could vaguely hear someone calling my name as I regained consciousness and slowly remembered where I was.

The good news was that the surgery was over.

"You did great," a kind nurse assured me as she patted my hand. "But your heart really raced during the surgery!"

When I was alert enough, I explained that, for me, a hospital produces a racing heart. She seemed to understand and mentioned that many people share my fear. Although I did not necessarily believe her, it was good to hear that I was not the only one reduced to a walking stress level whenever I entered a doctor's office and/or hospital.

Jennifer and Mimi were allowed in the room as the anesthesia continued to leave my system. I was very comforted by their presence but wanted nothing more than to simply go home. I concentrated on the fact that the outpatient surgery was over and I would soon be in front of my fireplace wearing a really cute gown that was not distinguished by a split down the back. However, I still felt the nagging fear of not yet knowing what the result of this lumpectomy would be.

Meanwhile, the nurses kept a watchful eye and told me I would be able to leave just as soon as my heart slowed to a normal pace.

Jennifer and Mimi both rolled their eyes! Yes, they actually rolled their eyes and explained to the nurse that my heart would not resume a normal rhythm until I was far away from the hospital.

I couldn't have said it better myself.

My surgeon entered the room and gave me the official okay to go home. He knew me well and understood the heart rhythm situation. I was free to leave but was to call, of course, if I had any problems. At that moment, the only problem I had was wondering whether or not I had the big "C."

Unfortunately, my surgery took place on December 23, just two days before Christmas. The lab was closing until December 27. Thus, I had an eternity to wonder about test results.

For the moment, I tried to focus on the fact that surgery was over and I was going home where my heart would beat normally again.

Besides, because of that eye-rolling incident, I planned on having Jennifer and Mimi wait on me hand and foot for the rest of the day.

✿✿✿✿✿

You can probably guess that after several days of agonizing uncertainty, my doctor called. This time he spoke with a brighter voice and actually used the "B" word – *BENIGN*. The lump was simply a benign mass that could have been part of me for many years. I did not care how long it had been there. I only cared that the doctor had used the "B" word to describe it. Benign! What a magnificent word!

So why have I babbled on about this experience?

Three reasons. First, many women do not hear the "B" word when their doctor calls. Each year, thousands of women learn that their battle with breast cancer is just beginning. It is a frightening battle whose outcome is very uncertain. We need to remember each of those fighting this disease and pray for strength and peace as they struggle.

Second, mammograms are important. While I certainly never wanted to receive the call that told me something had been found, it turned out well for me. But I never felt the lump and it would never have been detected without the mammogram. As embarrassing and bothersome as the procedure is, *it saves lives*. The good news is that most lumps are not cancerous. But the reassurance provided by a doctor is a gift beyond words.

Most importantly, in the face of my tremendous fear, I actually experienced peace in the days preceding my surgery. For me, that was downright miraculous!

I am not ashamed to say that I spent time on my knees after I received the call from my doctor. I was very afraid and knew that I needed peace. And I know the One who says, "Peace, be still," and calms the storm.

So in the bedroom of a home on Henderson Mill Road in Atlanta, Georgia, I fell to my knees and allowed the arms of my Heavenly Father to wrap me in His peace and His love. I prayed and I listened as God spoke words of peace to me. When I arose,

I recognized that a very real peace filled me that night and in the days prior to my surgery. Though my fear was present during the morning of my surgery, I do remember the unbelievable sense of peace I felt before that day.

The lesson is this. God could have very easily removed the lump from my breast. It would have been a true miracle. Many have experienced healings far more miraculous than this.

But God knew I needed a different miracle – the miracle of peace. And I received that miracle. I experienced the peace that passes all understanding; a peace that stood firm in the face of my worst fear and anxiety. Of course, I would have rejoiced had the lump magically disappeared, but that was not the miracle I needed. My miracle was peace . . . sweet peace . . . indescribable peace . . . the peace that indeed passes all understanding.

Have you experienced your own times of turmoil? If so, you understand how wonderful it is to relax, breathe deeply, and feel this precious gift.

What began as a terrifying experience ultimately taught me a lesson I desperately needed to learn . . . peace is ours, truly ours, if we only ask. Whatever your circumstance, whatever your fear, whatever you face today, please take the lesson I learned and accept it as your own.

God grants peace.

May the God of peace, abide in your heart and grant you serenity today and every day.

Mammograms Save Lives
For more information call
The American Cancer Society
1-800-ACS-2345
www.cancer.org

---

*Be careful for nothing;
but in every thing
by prayer and thanksgiving
let your requests be made known unto God.
And the peace of God,
which passeth all understanding,
shall keep your hearts and minds
through Christ Jesus.*

Philippians 4:6-7

The Arm Thing

Overcoming the Frustrations of Aging

I am doing it. Some of my friends are doing it. Strangers in public places are doing it. Perhaps you are even doing it right now.

It happens gradually. At first you may not realize the words of your favorite novel are growing fuzzy. You might not notice that you tilt your head backward during the Sunday worship service as you read the Scripture passage from your favorite Bible. You probably cannot recall the exact day your world began to grow hazy. Then, BOOM, one horrible day you catch yourself reading the Sunday paper with your arms stretched full length from your eyes. In fact, you consider sweetly asking your spouse to sprint the distance of a football field and hold the paper so that you can focus properly.

Congratulations, my friend! You have just done *The Arm Thing.*

Excuse me, but did you think you would be the only one to magically escape this familiar element of the aging process?

I did.

But, it gets worse.

I have actually laughed at other people doing *The Arm Thing.* Absolutely. And, of course, I vowed that it would never happen to me.

I remember when my husband, Jerry, first began *The Arm Thing*.

"Getting a little old, Jer?" I inquired with a lighthearted snicker. "Do you need those arms lengthened or should I sprint the distance of a football field and hold that paper so that you can focus properly?"

He grinned at me. Or was it a sneer?

But, it gets worse.

One day as Jerry and I walked through the aisles of our favorite Wal-Mart, he asked me to help him purchase a new watch.

"Why?" I asked. He already had a collection of several nice watches.

With a sheepish grin he explained that none of those watches met his current requirements. What requirements? First, the watch must have a round face. No ovals or squares or odd angular shapes. It had to be round. And large. Large enough for him to see it easily while preaching. (Please allow me to pause here to simply ask: Do preachers ever pay attention to their watches anyway?). Finally, the watch must have real numbers. No dots, slashes, or even Roman Numerals. Real numbers . . . . the 1, 2, 3, kind. Real numbers on a large round face.

Naturally I laughed and kidded him throughout the thirty minutes or so it took us to locate a watch that met all his requirements.

"So, is this the official timepiece of *The Arm Thing Generation*?" I joked.

He looked at me with a combination of tolerance, wisdom, and the assurance that, one day, I would have my own experience with *The Arm Thing*.

My husband, Jerry, passed away a few years ago and is not here to give me my comeuppance. I would gladly endure the jokes if I could have him back, but some things are out of my hands. Therefore, I think it only fair to admit the inevitable. During my forty-something years I've learned that no one escapes the pangs of aging – not even me. I joined *The Arm Thing Generation* several months ago and I am wearing my new glasses at this very moment.

One day not so long ago, I discovered to my horror that words were becoming fuzzy and I tilted my head backward when I read my Bible or any other book. Yea verily, I have wondered about asking various friends to sprint the distance of a football field and hold the newspaper for me. It has been quite a lesson in humility to learn that I am not ten-feet-tall and bulletproof when it comes to the aging process.

I know I should be thankful that my eye doctor told me just a few weeks ago, "I have good news, Cathy! You have no disease of the eye. All of this is simply typical of the aging process."

I'm still waiting for the good news.

If Jerry were here, he would laugh with me, tease me lightheartedly, and tell me that life is forever filled with changes and challenges but that through them all, our eyes should always be on God.

You see, wisdom also comes with the aging process.

I really must go now because I actually think I might cry. Besides, I need to go to Wal-Mart and buy a new watch . . . .

Cast me not off
In the time of my old age;
Forsake me not
When my strength faileth.

Psalm 71:9

I Didn't Even Know His Name

| Overcoming Selfishness |

*M*y husband, Jerry, walked through the front door and sat his briefcase next to the tall grandfather clock. I was preparing supper and heard only part of the conversation.

"Who died?" I asked, trying to understand what he was saying.

"The man I've been telling you about. He's been sick for weeks," Jerry responded.

Then I remembered. An older man, a Veteran of World War II was a member of Jerry's church. Jerry loved this man and would sit for hours as the gentleman shared stories of his days amid the horror of war. Time and cancer, though, had overtaken the man's body and he had been close to death for several days. On this day, my husband sat with a family who had said their final good-bye to a beloved husband, father, and grandfather. My heart hurt for Jerry and for the family who had watched this loved one slip away. I, too, grieved for the man and I didn't even know his name.

"Cath, they want to have the funeral on April 5," Jerry told me in a tentative voice.

I turned to face Jerry and my attitude quickly changed.

"Surely this is a joke," I snapped. Surely my husband would not spend April 5, our FIRST wedding anniversary, performing a funeral for this man I did not even know. After all, we would celebrate our first anniversary only once, and I certainly did not intend for that celebration to take place in a funeral home. In my anger I became convinced that this man had timed his death just to destroy our anniversary plans.

Was I being selfish? Certainly. But please do not judge me too harshly. As a preacher's wife I quickly grew accustomed to planning my life around a church calendar. That was fine – most of the time. But it seemed that funerals, weddings, church meetings, or last minute details were forever interrupting a vacation or day off or special evening together. And now my very first wedding anniversary was being ruined because of the death of this man – and I didn't even know his name.

So, I proceeded to pout and throw a rather exquisite "preacher's wife temper tantrum." After all, I was genuinely angry. I had waited my entire lifetime to celebrate a wedding anniversary and I did not want to be cheated out of the experience. Plus, I knew my emotional display would probably be good for an extra present or two!

Regardless of my tantrum, I realized what the priority would be on that April 5. Receiving a dozen pink roses that morning did make it far easier for me to dress for the funeral. And, Jerry had promised me a romantic dinner at our favorite restaurant. Obviously, our first anniversary would not be a total failure.

Jerry was very quiet as he drove to the funeral home that April afternoon.

"He probably feels really guilty about our anniversary," I thought to myself. But as we walked into the funeral home hand-in-hand, I recognized that Jerry's thoughts were on greater issues – his genuine friendship with this man and his role as minister to a grieving family.

To my own amazement I felt my anger melting as I faced a flag-draped coffin flanked by two young soldiers dressed nobly in Class A Army uniforms complete with caps and white gloves. They stood crisply at attention, their eyes fixed in time. A simple arrangement of red and white flowers adorned with a large blue bow sat nobly in front of the stately bronze coffin. A quiet dignity filled the room as a mixture of veterans, displaying the regalia of their own military service, paid tribute to one of their own. There were hugs, tears, and talk of battles won and lost. There were remembrances of friends who never came home. But there was laughter as well. Having never attended a military funeral, I was awe-struck by the unity and love displayed by this extended armed forces family.

Once Jerry offered his final prayer with the family, three soldiers and one non-commissioned officer stepped forward in unison to accompany the coffin to the chapel. Inside the chapel, these young soldiers offered a slow salute to the man who had fought so bravely for our country. The service was a beautiful mixture of respect, honor, and patriotism. It was a heartfelt celebration, not only for the one who had died, but also for all who love this country.

Full Military Honors were present at the gravesite as well. Following Jerry's words of comfort, the four uniformed soldiers gave one final slow salute to the man in the coffin. Then, while two of the soldiers watched attentively, the remaining two silently folded the American flag neatly into its familiar triangular shape. Not a word was spoken but, in the quiet, I was not surprised to hear the rattle of tissues as tears were wiped away from sad eyes. To my surprise, one of those tissues belonged to me. Unashamed of my falling tears, I watched as a soldier presented this flag to the man's widow and whispered words of comfort "on behalf of a grateful nation."

My eyes flooded and I reached for another tissue.

Wiping my eyes, I flinched as in the distance, four uniformed riflemen fired shots overhead. As the echo of gunfire

41

faded, the mournful wail of "Taps" was played by a young man with tears in his own eyes.

As the crowd dispersed, I walked silently to grasp the hand of my husband on our first wedding anniversary. With tears streaming down my face, my thoughts of presents and flowers fled to the back of my mind. Silently I scolded myself for my selfishness and the memory of my rather exquisite "preacher's wife temper tantrum."

I had just learned, in a very poignant manner, the way in which our priorities can so easily go astray. I had just learned, in a very poignant manner, what a blessing it is to live in the United States of America, and how grateful I am to those who have made freedom a reality for me.

I wept for a hero that day. And I didn't even know his name.

*Let nothing be done
through strife or vanity;
but in lowliness of mind
let each esteem others
better than themselves.*

Philippians 2:3

"Yes, But We're Rich!"

Overcoming Greed

She was a ten-year-old with an ATTITUDE . . . A little elementary diva who made her presence known simply by walking into a room.

Emily wore designer clothes, designer shoes, and dressed perfectly down to, I suppose, her designer underwear. Her bedroom was amply filled with beautiful things – a canopied bed, of course, covered with a pink lace comforter topped with an array of expensive dolls and teddy bears. Her bedside table held a white French telephone and her own private phone line. Across the room sat an entertainment center featuring a large television and VCR plus a wide selection of video games. A large shelf held a pricey sound system with a multitude of tapes and CDs. Emily's desk boasted the biggest and best mega-computer featuring all the bells and whistles of processing technology.

Much of her time was spent in dance and gymnastics classes. Emily's diet was already closely monitored by a mother determined that her child would develop the perfect body for wearing her designer clothes. An A student, Emily attended an exclusive private school. Even at her young age, Emily's parents had a life charted for her that would include an elite finishing school and an Ivy League college where she would meet and marry a proper husband who would continue to pamper her according to this fashion. Emily already possessed an impressive financial portfolio that, undoubtedly, outranked the budgets of several small countries! In short, Emily's life was affluent and privileged. As early as age ten Emily was acutely aware of her riches and enjoyed demanding the privileges she felt accompanied her fortunate lifestyle.

But on a cool Sunday morning one October, Emily, still the ten-year-old child, simply wanted to hold the bowl during the children's sermon at the 11:00 a.m. worship service.

Leading the children's sermon during a Sunday morning worship service can be a challenge. I am forever flexing my creative muscles to, hopefully, maintain the attention of a church filled with restless children. That fall morning I was illustrating a point that simply required my squeezing a tube of toothpaste into an ordinary bowl.

"Would someone like to help me by holding this bowl?" I asked. Approximately sixty hands flew up and I called on Garrett, whose hand I saw first. Garrett held the bowl with great pizzazz – he could have qualified as a professional "bowl holder" – and the children's sermon proceeded with no problem.

As I was leaving the church that morning, though, Emily stormed down the aisle. Without going into great detail, let me just say that she was not exhibiting a warm and happy attitude! With her hand planted firmly on her right hip, she stomped her small foot in anger.

"Cathy," she demanded, "Cathy, I want to know why you didn't let me hold the bowl this morning."

I cringed. How could a mere ten-year-old suddenly make me feel totally responsible for everything from the Kennedy Assassination to world hunger? Answering her in the most pleasant voice I could muster, I replied, "Well, Emily, I saw Garrett's hand first so I called on him."

While this explanation seemed quite logical to me, it simply was not sufficient for Emily, a child accustomed to privileges both great and small.

So on that cool Sunday morning, Emily glared at me with an exquisite scowl, and bellowed, "YES, BUT WE'RE RICH!" (And this is a direct quote.)

Yes, but we're rich?

She was only ten years old! The only thing more astounding than her statement was my complete speechlessness. I had no snappy reply, no great theological discourse, not even an incoherent stutter. As I stood in shocked silence, Emily quickly turned and marched out the door.

My eyes closed in panic as I envisioned the headlines of Monday's Atlanta Journal: *"CHRISTIAN EDUCATOR SUED FOR INFLICTING PSYCHOLOGICAL DAMAGE ON CHILD DURING UGLY BOWL-HOLDING INCIDENT."*

I expected the legal papers to be served before sundown.

So, where is Emily today? I don't know, but I often wonder about her. I wish I could sit and talk with her for a while. I would say some things I should have said before she turned and walked away that October day.

Being older and wiser now, I would talk to Emily about what it really means to be rich and I would urge her to choose her riches carefully. I would pray that *FAITH* would be her first choice. I would tell Emily that, through faith, God will meet her every need because no one is richer than God. I would tell her that life can be hard and that bank accounts, designer clothes, and canopied beds will not keep her from feeling the hurt of living in an imperfect world. I would tell her that through faith, she will be comforted and granted peace during those inescapable times when life makes no sense at all. I would tell her that through faith, she will know that a loving God walks with her during times of both victory and heartbreak. I would tell her that through faith and prayer, there is nothing she could not share with God, the Creator of our vast universe. I would tell her that through faith, she will experience guidance when her steps are uncertain, strength when she is weary, and forgiveness when she has sinned.

I would tell her that through faith, she will experience the unconditional love of God.

Most importantly, I would tell Emily that through faith in God and belief in His promises, she will inherit a place in God's Heavenly Kingdom. And not even a platinum credit card can purchase the greatest treasure of all – the gift of eternal life.

I cannot forget Emily, the ten-year-old with an attitude. She was rich and it showed in her clothes, her room, and her way of life. Emily is older now and I pray she has indeed chosen wisely and is rich in faith and in the knowledge of God.

You have to make that choice, too. Have you chosen wisely?

Got faith? Then celebrate, my friends, because you are undeniably rich – and you have an inheritance coming that is out of this world!

*Hearken, my beloved brethren,
hath not God chosen
the poor of this world
rich in faith,
and heirs of the kingdom
which He promised to them
that love Him?*

James 2:5

Of Futures and Fortune Cookies

Overcoming Fear of the Future

The day had been a long one filled with deadlines and headaches. Driving home, I could not determine what I felt most – fatigue or hunger.

It was late and, having neither the supplies nor the desire to cook at home, I sought a nearby restaurant. Spying a green neon *OPEN* sign, I made a quick right turn into the parking lot of the local Chinese eatery. Just then, my quick Tuesday evening meal was suddenly transformed into a pleasant dining experience as I unexpectedly encountered my good friends, Joe and Elizabeth Baltes, at the restaurant door.

"What a great surprise!" we exclaimed as we were seated together. If we had tried to plan dinner together, we probably would never have found an evening to fit our three busy schedules. So enjoying this rare time together, we talked nonstop over Egg Drop Soup, Sesame Beef, and Walnut Chicken. Our conversation consisted of the typical stuff of friendships – talking of our work and home, sharing of our joys and frustrations and dreams. Sprinkled among our words was just the right dose of laughter to further strengthen the cords of friendship.

As the plates emptied and our stomachs filled, the waiter delivered to our table a dish filled with fresh orange slices and fortune cookies. I was the second to select a fortune cookie and I did so with great pomp and ceremony.

"Okay," I said aloud, "I really want good fortune and some great words of wisdom." The truth be known, I was going through a rough time and desperately needed some good fortune and great words of wisdom. After my short speech, I selected a fortune cookie in the center of the pile and popped open the wrapper. Knowing some of my recent frustrations, Joe and Elizabeth watched with anticipation as I eagerly cracked the cookie and prepared to receive the knowledge, insight, and hope it contained – the answer to life's deep mysteries condensed onto one tiny slip of paper.

But, alas, my fortune cookie did not contain a tiny slip of paper laced with profound thoughts. In fact, my fortune cookie was completely bare. Get it? Vacant. Blank. Totally void of wise words, hope for the future, or deep insights into life's mysteries. That arrogant little cookie spoke volumes to me.

"What an appropriate tribute to my life right now," I thought to myself. "I can't even get a break from a fortune cookie!"

Joe and Elizabeth laughed, of course. And after an adequate degree of pouting, I laughed as well. The waiter even brought me a new fortune cookie with a wonderful message: *"You will receive many blessings and your trouble will soon pass."* Great! But even those words did not remove the sting of my original empty fortune cookie.

I am smart enough to recognize that my future is not determined by a few words printed on a tiny slip of paper stuffed into a fortune cookie. But it does at least make me feel better when my cookie has a nice message inside. At that moment, though, even a rotten message would have been better than an empty fortune cookie that seemingly indicated I had no future at all.

Well, I've been thinking about my fortune cookie since that Tuesday night (yes, I do have better things to do, but stick with me for a moment longer).

Perhaps I received the wrong message from that empty cookie. Instead of believing my future is *nothing*, why shouldn't I believe my future can be *anything* – with possibilities so infinite, eternal, and wonderful they cannot be limited to a small slip of paper stuffed into a fortune cookie?

My future is as grand as my dreams and hopes and wishes. My future is as vast as the God who guides me toward it. And regardless of the bad times of years ago, of last week, or of yesterday, a new day begins with each sunrise. I can make what I will of that day, knowing that Jesus Christ came to give me abundant life – an *anything* future instead of a *nothing* future.

The same is true for each of us, of course. God has a plan for you – an *anything* future – just as He has for me. And though it may not be completely clear at the moment, God beckons us into that future of infinite possibilities. Best of all, God walks beside us as we realize our future!

The next step is yours and mine. Is it time to forget empty fortune cookies and doomsday prophecies of a nothing future? Yes! Is it time to forget the hurts and doubts from painful yesterdays that continue to haunt us? Absolutely! Is it time to take our place and walk confidently into that future God holds for us? Definitely!

Ours can be an *anything* future or a *nothing* future. The decision is ours.

God has extended His hand. Go ahead – accept it and walk boldly into your *anything* future!

> *"For I know the plans I have for you,"*
> *declares the Lord,*
> *"plans to prosper you*
> *and not to harm you,*
> *plans to give you a*
> *future and a hope."*
>
> *Jeremiah 29:11*

Life . . . A Laughing Matter!

*A*fter weeks of planning, everything was ready for the Sunrise Service. The setting was a beautiful green pasture surrounded by rolling meadows and a rippling creek. The music was well rehearsed. A tall wooden cross adorned with colorful spring flowers stood next to the podium. Volunteers were in place to assist with parking and seating arrangements as the crowds began to gather.

And then the rains came.

Umbrellas blossomed and the once picturesque pasture quickly became a quagmire where steps were uncertain on the slippery ground. Expensive shoes made squishing noises and attractive suits, dresses, and even hats were splashed with mud. The mood changed quickly and many twisted their faces in anger and uttered very "un-Easter-like" words.

And I laughed!

I laughed – not from lunacy (?) or a warped sense of humor. I laughed at how amusing we humans are. Of course, this special service would have been much more pleasant in the dry warmth of the early morning sun. But, compared to the resurrection of Christ, why should a few raindrops hold such significance? I have to admit that I've been laughing a bit more since that Easter morning because those raindrops reminded me to measure my daily frustrations against the backdrop of eternity.

51

Please do not misunderstand. I am painfully aware that some things are not laughing matters. But can't we try to keep life in its proper perspective and remember to laugh at the silly things we take all too seriously?

Learn to laugh, for instance, when the business call is accidentally forwarded to the wrong person or the copy machine jams before the big corporate meeting. Or when you drive a yellow pollen-covered car each spring and sneeze at all the wrong times. Or when our northern friends -- those doggone Yankees -- joke about how an inch of snow paralyzes the entire city of Atlanta. Or when you find three typographical errors *after* the bulletin has been printed and folded. Or when you accidentally mark the wrong date on your calendar and arrive for a lunch date one day too late. Or you spill your glass of tea at a fancy restaurant. Or your son shares an embarrassing story with the whole church during the children's sermon. Or the dog jumps up to greet you with mud on his feet. Laugh at getting older and growing ear hair, nose hair, chin hair, gray hair, or no hair. Laugh with the child who ponders whether God is married to Mother Nature. Laugh when you spend weeks planting and fertilizing new grass and then grumble about mowing it once it grows. Laugh when you develop the hiccups in the middle of a job interview. Laugh when, despite all your plans and best intentions, the world rains on your parade.

Laugh, my friends, because this is the stuff of life. While these frustrations are very real, they are only temporary and nothing in light of the message of Easter.

Shout with joy because the empty tomb is greater than an ugly wooden cross and the promise of eternal life is greater than the frustration of this life. The stone has been rolled away and Christ is risen. Death has been swallowed up in victory and while grief is truly agonizing, it cannot erase the promise of life everlasting.

The rains came this Easter, just as the rains inevitably come into every life. And though the ground may be unsteady and our steps may falter for a while, we know we will once again stand tall because Christ has overcome the world!

Christ is risen. He is risen, indeed.

Can you think of a better reason to laugh?

The angel said to the women,
Fear not
for I know that ye
seek Jesus, which was crucified.
He is not here:
for He is risen, as he said.
Come, see the place
where the Lord lay.

Matthew 28:5-6

Cathy Lee Phillips

Never A Home

Overcoming Life in a Less-Than-Perfect Home

At the end of the road in a dark wooded glen
A lonely house stood where a home should have
been.
Made of timber and nails, such a typical dwelling,
The story of life within most compelling.

For the promise and hope of that house newly-born
Turned to anger and hurt, became bitter and torn
Like those living inside unable to see
They were only mere strangers where a family should be.

The unfulfilled vows of the husband and wife
Divided and conquered, then took root in each life
Of the children born into the house in the glen,
The sad, lonely house where a home should have been.

The house held all of the usual things –
But none of the comfort a home's meant to bring.
For along with the chairs, the tables, the beds,
Lived the deep painful scars of harsh words that were said.

The house heard no sweet sounds of love, heard no laughter,
Those valuable things we all seem to seek after.
There is only so much that a mere house can do
When its efforts are choked by the deeds of a few

Who never learned how to bring sweet love and grace
Into the heart of that sad, pain-filled place.
Instead, heeding only their anger and blindness
No one ever took time to understand kindness.

Well, the years now have passed and the timbers are gone,
But the house in the glen still sadly lives on
In the hearts of the ones who once dwelt there within
The lonely old house where a home should have been.

Yet in an obscure tiny section of yard
A bulb fights its way through the ground, frozen hard.
And when it breaks through the cold wintry sod,
It grows in the light with its face turned toward God.

Hope still lives on, it seems to relate,
And love conquers jealousy, anger, and hate.
All you can be is not what you were then
In the sad, lonely house in the dark wooded glen.

The pain of the past and the hurt you have known
Have molded and shaped you -- even there you have grown.
Take the lessons you learned, though painful they be
And use them to plant a new family tree.

Heaven's blessings abound; you will have a new chance
To love and to laugh, to grow and to dance.
Now go build your own house, and with God as your guide
You'll at last find your home and true family inside.

*Whosoever heareth
these sayings of mine,
and doeth them,
I will liken him unto a wise man,
which built his house upon a rock:
and the rain descended,
and the floods came,
and the winds blew,
and beat upon that house;
and it fell not:
for it was founded upon a rock.*

Matthew 7:24-25

One Hairy Dog and Two Crispy Biscuits

Overcoming the Fear of Letting Go

O kay, I'll be the first to admit that Martha Stewart does not live at my house. She doesn't even know my address!

I do, though, have my "homemaker moments." While I am not the same *Doris Domestic* I was when married, my home has never once been reported to the Health Department. And I can usually go for a week or so without setting off the fire alarm when cooking. The fact is, I cook very little these days. Those who are living solo will understand that it is much easier to eat out than to prepare a meal for one. So I am more than happy to spend my time in other pursuits.

Breathe easy, Martha Stewart, your reputation is safe!

Lack of practice is, perhaps, the reason my biscuits burned one summer Saturday morning. Actually, I hate to say *burned.* Let's just say the biscuits were, well, *crispy.* I placed them in the oven but turned my attention to something else. I returned to the kitchen only when I sniffed the unmistakable smell of, well, crispy biscuits. While they were not completely ruined, I decided not to expend my quota of carbs and fat grams on these particular biscuits.

No problem! I simply popped two other biscuits in the oven and watched carefully as they baked to golden perfection. My breakfast was only delayed by a few minutes.

One point of clarification may be necessary here. Did you think that, perhaps, I made these biscuits from scratch? Goodness, no! Martha Stewart does not live here, remember? These biscuits came from the frozen food section at Publix. They remained rock-solid in my freezer until I popped them into the oven. Thirteen minutes later (or eighteen minutes for the crispy variety), I had warm biscuits ready to be filled with butter and jelly – and not one trace of dough on my hands!

Is this a great country, or what?

When I finished breakfast that Saturday morning, I faced a dilemma. What is the proper means of disposing of two crispy biscuits? I decided that instead of placing them in the garbage, I would give them to Shadow.

Shadow is the newest addition to the Phillips household. He is a golden retriever mix adopted from the local animal shelter. My previous dog, Victory, passed away last year on Christmas Eve. Victory was a special dog and it was very hard to lose my faithful canine companion, especially on Christmas Eve.

Though I waited several months, I quickly realized that I wanted another dog.

"What kind of dog do you want?" people asked.

"I don't know," I responded. "But I will know him when I see him."

One warm day, my friend, Caroline Sosebee, and her two sons, Brandon and Trace, decided it was time for me to find a new dog. We piled into Caroline's new just-off-the-lot van and invaded the local animal shelter. After examining all sorts of dogs, my eyes landed on the creature I knew was destined to be my dog. He was happy, cute, and friendly – everything I wanted. The only problem was the wicked woman who saw him first and threw her body between the dog and me.

Not wanting me to start a brawl at the local animal shelter, Caroline suggested that I find another dog.

"No," I insisted. "This is my dog."

I watched helplessly as this wicked woman took my dog outside to *bond* with him before finalizing the adoption. Was it horrible of me to pray the dog would bite her? No serious injury, of course. A tiny nick with a small loss of blood would be sufficient.

Moments later, woman brought my dog back into the kennel. Knowing that I had the dog in my sights, she said to me, "He is a fence climber and I will just not have that."

I was delighted! I have a six-foot wooden fence. And I was thankful that the dog was going to be mine without the animal actually having to bite the woman.

The Sosebee clan and I took the dog outside to an enclosed "bonding area." Brandon and I played with and petted the dog. Trace, afraid of the abundance of canine energy, curled up in Caroline's lap and gave his approval of the dog from a distance. While I was bonding with the dog, so was Brandon. For I moment I thought I might actually have to adopt both Brandon and the dog because they were quickly becoming a matched set. In fact, Brandon volunteered to sit with the dog while I completed paperwork and wrote the check that made him the official dog of the Phillips household. In a matter of minutes we had placed the golden puppy on a blanket in the back of Caroline's van and were happily on our way home.

I was so thankful Caroline had volunteered her van in which to transport the dog. It was far roomier than my car. And, I'll admit, I was especially thankful to be in Caroline's van when the dog experienced a case of motion sickness and "baptized" the vehicle. Even though we stopped and cleaned everything, that "new car" smell certainly disappeared that day.

Driving quite a bit slower, we crept home without further incident. I placed the dog in the fence where Brandon continued to play happily with him. In view of their special connection, I conferred upon Brandon the title of the *Doggie Godfather.* He was thrilled – Brandon, that is. I don't think the dog noticed.

Within a few minutes we named the dog *Shadow* because he shadowed me wherever I went. He stayed right with me and was obviously quite content with his new home. He's been a happy puppy since that day.

❁❁❁❁❁

But, back to the biscuits.

Shadow is always happy to see me. He is even happier when I come bearing food. I held out the first biscuit and Shadow sniffed it then quickly seized it from my hand. Of course, I also love this dog because he is non-judgmental and did not care that the biscuit was a tad burned (well, crispy!).

I waited for Shadow to gobble the biscuit but was interested when he marched around the yard while holding the biscuit tightly in his mouth. Intrigued (and almost insulted), I realized he was going to hide his biscuit. I supposed it would be a great mid-afternoon snack when his daily serving of Wal-Mart Old Roy Dog Food had been digested. Shadow marched from one end of the yard to the other, surveying, sniffing, and finally locating a spot to conceal his biscuit. On the right side of the yard, next to the fence, Shadow began to dig a hole.

He dug with his front paws and burrowed with his nose, never letting the biscuit leave his mouth. But he suddenly stopped, obviously not satisfied with the location.

Becoming quite impatient I spoke to Shadow in a stern voice, "Go ahead! Eat the biscuit. I have another one waiting for you in the kitchen."

The dog ignored me and, again, marched around the yard. He started and stopped his digging several more times, causing me further irritation.

"Eat the biscuit, you crazy dog. Eat it and I will let you have the other biscuit, too. Doggone it!"

Again, the dog ignored me. I went back inside, finished cleaning the kitchen, and about an hour later presented Shadow with the second crispy biscuit, which he eagerly accepted.

❂❂❂❂❂

So what did I learn on an ordinary Saturday morning from one hairy dog and two crispy biscuits? Like me, Shadow had a problem letting go. He held on to what he had, not realizing that by giving up the first biscuit, he could have a second one.

There are times when I need to let go – of past hurts, of situations over which I have no control, of panic over what the next day might bring, and of routines that provide security but no challenge or growth. Often times we may be miserable, yet comfortable, and too afraid to let go of the familiar even though God may have something far better awaiting us. Just think of the challenges and adventures that await me – and you – if we have the courage to move beyond our comfort zones. Alas, how often I have been content with one small crispy biscuit when God wanted to bless me with so much more. All that I needed was simply to let go of what I thought was my security and instead, truly trust God to take care of me.

Letting go is hard work. I know. I've had to do it all too often. It is frightening to let go of a sure thing when you do not know what, if anything, will take its place.

The good news, though, is that I have never surrendered anything to God without being blessed in return. God does not want us to settle for crispy biscuits when delicious, golden ones are available. He wants our lives to be abundant and filled with the greatest He has to offer. God wants us to be willing to let go when it is best for us, having faith that something bigger and better awaits us.

We are a lot like the Israelites. We must have the courage to let go of the Egypt that binds us before we will ever see a Promised Land flowing with milk and honey.

Shadow enjoyed two crispy biscuits that Saturday morning because he finally found the courage to let go of the first biscuit.

Lord, help me to embrace the blessings you have in store for me. When the time is right, grant me the courage to let go of the "comfortable" and trust You to guide me to the "wonderful!"

Eye hath not seen,
nor ear heard,
neither have entered into the
heart of man,
the things which God hath
prepared for them that
love Him.

I Corinthians 2:9

Dance of the Blue Butterfly

Overcoming the Sting of Death

"When it happens, will you find a way to let me know you are okay?"

She was fifty-two years old and after a sixteen-year battle with a horrible disease, her life was ending. Marked with the scars and bruises of prolonged medical treatment, her body was too weak to sustain life much longer. But she was very much alive at that moment, and in an ordinary room at Emory University Hospital in Atlanta, she wanted to talk – about life and death and faith – the things that are really important at such a time. I sat on the edge of the bed and held my mother's hand as we talked and laughed and cried.

"Nothing flashy. No lightening bolts or earthquakes." My request was not made in jest. It was a statement of faith. I believed fully in life after death – in *her* life after *her* death. I wanted, perhaps, to strengthen her with my confidence. At the same time, I wanted my faith to comfort me in that frightening moment.

"Just a simple sign," I continued, "one that will let me know that God is taking good care of you."

"I will," she quietly promised.

We continued our conversation, sharing the ordinary and the profound, the frustrations of the day, the mysteries of the universe, private jokes, and an appropriate touch of gossip. In the long run, we shared far more laughter than tears.

My mother had been desperately ill for sixteen years. In fact, there were times I could barely remember what my mother was like before the disease. Most days, in fact, I felt more intimately acquainted with Wegener's Granulomatosis, her rare and gruesome disease, than with my mother herself. Her appearance had dramatically changed. Her personality had been forever altered. Yet the pain of those sixteen years did not matter that afternoon in her hospital room. All that mattered was the moment and those matters of life and death and faith -- and my question.

"When it happens, will you find a way to let me know you are okay?"

"I will," she promised.

A few days later, in the early hours of an August morning, my mother left behind her broken body and journeyed into her new life. I celebrated for her, secure in the faith that only her diseased body had died. My mother lived on, I knew, pain-free and strong for the first time in many years.

At her request, my husband, Jerry, made preparations for her memorial service. He was not only her son-in-law; Jerry was her pastor as well. As Jerry planned, I prepared a bulletin that included an order of worship and a few words about my mother's life. Once the inside of the bulletin was complete, I searched for an appropriate cover page. I had an abundance of artwork – crosses and flowers, birds and sunrises, words of Scripture and comfort. Nothing, though, seemed appropriate. Sensing my indecision, Jerry made the choice for me.

"Use this butterfly," he stated, holding a plain black and white graphic.

"It is so ordinary," I said. I wished for a photograph of a huge, brilliant blue butterfly. Blue was my mother's favorite color, I recalled.

"Use the butterfly," Jerry stated again. "It is the Christian symbol of resurrection, of rebirth, of new life."

Yes, the butterfly would be appropriate. It seemed that my mother had spent sixteen long years in a dark cocoon. At her death, though, she had been released from her cocoon of disease into a wonderful new life. So, placing the butterfly prominently on the cover, I completed the bulletin.

Jerry and I visited the church early the next morning and as he arranged his Bible and notes on the pulpit, I placed the bulletins for the ushers to distribute. Having attended to all the details, it was time to leave the little country church to travel to the funeral home.

As we stepped toward the car, Jerry suddenly seized my hand. "Don't move, Cathy, and look quickly!" he whispered.

On the hood of our car stood a brilliant butterfly. It was a splendid, majestic creature. A strikingly beautiful *blue* butterfly, completely blue except for the black markings accenting its tiny body. With its wings open wide, the small creature strolled gracefully atop the car for several minutes. Even as we walked closer, the butterfly remained on the hood.

I was amazed! Don't butterflies normally fly away in fear? This blue butterfly, though, seemed at peace and completely unafraid. Jerry and I stood transfixed for what seemed an eternity before the blue butterfly calmly spread its wings and took flight.

We watched intently as, dipping and diving with the wind, it flew unrestrained into the sunlight. Jerry held me tightly as this miraculous affirmation of resurrection unfolded before us in the form of a tiny blue butterfly. So simple, yet so profound in its significance. My mother had finally escaped her cocoon and entered into a new life with Christ. I knew that beyond any doubt.

As mysterious and frightening as it is, death is certainly not the end of life. It is merely a gateway to eternity.

Smiling and crying at once, I realized my mother had kept her promise. I turned my thankful heart toward the butterfly. It gently flew into the August sky, waltzing and gliding with the breeze, dancing the dance of life.

> *For this corruptible*
> *must put on incorruption,*
> *and this mortal*
> *must put on immortality . . .*
> *then shall be brought to pass*
> *the saying that is written,*
> *Death is swallowed up in victory*
>
> *I Corinthians 15:53-55*

Empty Chairs and Empty Hearts

Overcoming Holiday Grief

W hile I have never done the math, I am quite sure I have spent more than my share of Thanksgiving holidays in hospital rooms. Though I have never been a patient, I have been the daughter or wife of a patient. Hospital personnel always tried to make the day as festive as possible. Yet nothing kept me from being acutely aware of the fact that I was spending my holiday in a hospital – a place I did not want to be on an ordinary day, much less on a holiday.

Oddly enough, my mother taught me to prepare turkey and dressing during one of her many Thanksgiving stays at Atlanta's Emory University Hospital. She was in Intensive Care following surgery one year when it was obvious she would not be home for Thanksgiving. In order to keep life as "normal" as possible, she walked me through each step of preparing her lip-smacking turkey, dressing, and gravy. I took notes on a cheap sheet of notebook paper provided by a nurse.

As suspected, my mother remained in the hospital on Thanksgiving, but I did a respectable job of replicating her turkey, dressing, and gravy. At the very least, I was reasonably sure it was better than hospital food!

You may be surprised to learn that, once upon a time, I was quite "domestic." In fact, for most of my married life I prepared turkey, dressing, and gravy, as Jerry and I fed family and friends each year. While the food tasted fine, the holiday was no holiday for me because I spent it tied to the kitchen. I know many women who still do this – many of whom will be feeding *you* this Thanksgiving or Christmas!

One year, though, Jerry was in the hospital on Thanksgiving Day due to rejection related to his heart transplant. I was depressed about the circumstances but I comforted myself with the thought that at least I did not have to cook a big meal. In fact, I envisioned a gala Thanksgiving dinner at Waffle House or some equally fancy establishment that might be open on the holiday.

Though Waffle House would have been sufficient, I discovered a wonderful innovation in the food industry that had developed during those years I was stirring gravy at home. The Thanksgiving Buffet! Friends who dropped by the hospital that holiday introduced me to this wonderful creation. Have you tried it? It is great! Simply plop down your money and you receive a ticket to more food than you could eat in a million years. And here's the best part – you stuff yourself and then simply walk away. No shopping! No cooking! No cleaning!

Is this a great country or what?

Several years ago I lost my husband, Jerry. I was angry and had no desire to spend hours preparing the traditional turkey, dressing, and gravy. Not only had I lost my husband, I lost my *tradition* – the familiar and comfortable routine we had created that gave me a sense of belonging and continuity. What took its place was an immense depression that left me with no desire to entertain or even accept any of the many invitations I received to celebrate with others. I had no direction but I had plenty of bitterness. I missed my husband. I missed the security Jerry and I enjoyed in our own home. I missed doing things the way we had done them in the past. I even missed my gravy!

Even after all these years, I still have not developed another tradition for the holidays. Therefore, like so many who have experienced tremendous loss, my holidays are bittersweet and can be days to be *endured* instead of *enjoyed*. I write this not for sympathy, but for sharing truth with those who may be experiencing the pain of loss that only increases during the Thanksgiving and Christmas holidays. Perhaps these words will help you feel more "normal" in the midst of your holiday grief -- they come from my own depth of experience.

Do not feel sorry for me, though, because there are many people for whom the holidays are difficult. Good people lose family and friends every day. Consider the tragic events of September 11, 2001, the loss of thousands of lives due to a terrorist attack, and the thousands who will be facing their first holiday season without a loved one. Grief is universal. You grieve greatly when you have loved greatly. This is normal. Your emotion does not indicate a lack of faith or a weakness of character.

Many suffer each year from the "Empty Chair Syndrome," that acute pain felt when the holidays are dominated by grief and loss. The "Empty Chair Syndrome" is especially prevalent during the first or second holiday following a death. However, please realize that the grief never fully leaves you. It is quite normal to still feel the pain of loss many years later when, once again, you are reminded that someone you loved deeply is no longer sitting at the table.

Whether your custom is Mom's turkey and dressing at home or the convenient Thanksgiving buffet, there is still the gut-wrenching awareness that someone is missing and your life will never be the same. Not only has someone special been lost, so has the sense of security and comfort the holidays are supposed to bring. Your tradition is gone and your life will undergo a tremendous adjustment.

For those who are experiencing holidays dominated by loss and grief, the following is dedicated to you. For those who have not yet experienced the "Empty Chair Syndrome," consider yourself a lucky person. But, as a kindness, why not pass these thoughts along to someone who is struggling during the holidays?

- **Be kind to yourself.** Recognize that while these days are filled with joy for many, you have experienced a loss that has forever altered your life. Life goes on and many people do not understand your hurt and your struggle. Pamper yourself a bit with extra sleep, a massage, visits with good friends, or other things that bring you comfort.
- **Be in charge of how you observe the holidays.** There is no right or wrong way of doing this. Many well-meaning friends will insist that you be a part of their celebration. If you would enjoy this, please join them. However, if you are afraid of being overly emotional and feel more comfortable spending quiet time alone, do so. Make your own decision as long as it is a responsible decision. Take charge and do what is best for you.
- **Make some changes if you wish.** With the loss of someone special, your life has changed. Your traditions have also changed. So why not make some new traditions? Instead of staying home, take the family on a trip to the mountains or on a holiday cruise (budget

willing, of course). Enjoy that holiday buffet at a favorite restaurant or hotel for a change of scenery. By doing something entirely different, you may begin to build new traditions.

- **Consider doing something special for someone else.** You are not the only person hurting and you can receive a great deal by giving to others. Donate a gift in memory of your loved one, give money to charity, volunteer to help feed the hungry, adopt a needy family, or invite a single person to share the day with you.

- **Remember the significance of the holiday season.** Thanksgiving is for giving thanks. Give thanks for the time you had with this very special person. Christmas heralds the coming of Jesus Christ, the Son of God, into the world. Through Christ we have salvation and the assurance of being reunited with the person we miss so terribly. Celebrate this assurance and allow it to comfort you in your painful and lonely moments.

- **Speak about the person you loved.** Use his or her name lovingly and recall special memories. This person was a very important part of your life. It would be silly to act as though the person never existed. Talking about your loved one may make others uncomfortable at first. But, this person was very a very significant part of your life so speak proudly of the times you shared, the memories you built, and the lessons you learned from the one you loved.

- **Do not let anyone take your grief away from you.** Grief is a natural response to loss and, again, you will grieve greatly because you loved greatly. Those who have not experienced loss may be uncomfortable by your tears, but tears are also a normal part of grieving. Do not allow anyone to make you feel that your grief shows a lack of faith. Remember that Jesus wept at the tomb of His friend, Lazarus, even though Jesus knew He would raise Lazarus from the dead. Do not allow anyone to make you feel you are weak or wrong by experiencing the full range of your emotions. You are grieving and these feelings are normal elements of the grieving process. In fact, you may help educate those who, inevitably, will experience grief themselves. Be patient with yourself and do not feel you are going crazy or losing control. Be patient with others who have never experienced a loss of this magnitude, remembering that one day you will be able to bring comfort to them because of your own experience.

I pray these words may help you begin the healing process and better equip you to cope with what can be a very difficult time of year. Remember that, even on your darkest days, you do not walk alone.

Jesus wept.

John 11:35

Separate Journeys

*D*eath crept silently into your room,
gently extended His hand
and summoned you.
I could not stop Him.

As you journeyed with Death,
Grief summoned me,
locking me tightly in His cruel prison
where sobs quell the song of the whippoorwill
and waves of darkness drown the spirit.
My heart grows cold as a glacier.

Angels and roses may abound
but a clammy fog hides them from me.
I see only darkness.
I hear only questions.
I feel only loneliness.
I taste only bitter tears.

But, in mercy, Death tells you,
    "Speak to her."
        And through the fog you whisper to me,
        "Be at peace, Sweet," I hear you say,
           "A butterfly can still soar on an overcast day."

Your pilgrimage with Death continues,
    but not before you pause and, in love,
        tenderly unbolt Grief's prison door.

Ye now therefore have sorrow:
but I will see you again,
and your heart shall rejoice,
and your joy
no man taketh away from you

John 16:22

The Name Vignettes

Overcoming Doubts About God's Love
"Does He Really Know Who I Am?"

#1. A Cat Named "Firewood"

S am Stinson wanted only two things for his fourth
birthday – he wanted to go camping and he wanted
a kitten.

The camping trip was easy enough. Brian and Lynn,
Sam's parents, enjoyed camping. They even had a favorite spot at
a lake not far from their home. All camping supplies were packed
neatly in the garage and it would take only a matter of minutes to
load them onto the back of Brian's big purple truck. Lynn
purchased food and supplies for the campout, including an
appropriate birthday cake for a four-year-old little boy. All things
ready, the family set off for Sam's camping celebration at the
lake.

But, the cat.

That required a little more deliberation. While Brian and Lynn wanted to teach Sam the responsibility of owning a pet, they wondered whether Sam would soon lose interest in a four-legged fur ball and leave it for them to raise. But, it was hard to deny Sam's request. You see, Sam is their only child and, after all, it wasn't as if he had asked for a horse or anything extravagant. They had no other pets. Also (and I think this was the clincher!), Sam is as cute as they come! It would be awfully hard to say no to that child. With his father's big brown eyes and his mother's blonde hair, Sam is one precious four-year-old. I can only imagine the girls that will be circling the Stinson home when Sam celebrates birthday number sixteen!

So, as the three sat around the campsite that weekend, Sam eagerly blew out the candles on his birthday cake. Excited by the camping trip and his birthday adventure, Sam almost forgot his other wish until Brian fetched a small box from the back of the big purple truck. Sam jumped, clapped his hands, and rushed toward the box faster than Brian could gently remove the tiny kitten. Only a few weeks old, the little fur ball was solid black except for a white spot on her nose. Wriggling free from Brian, she pounced into Sam's waiting arms.

The bonding was immediate!

Sam stroked the kitten, held her tightly and listened to the rhythm of her soft purr. In only a few minutes she burrowed beneath Sam's chin and fell asleep.

"She's all mine?" Sam questioned. "You promise?"

Lynn assured Sam that the kitten was truly his very own. As his eyes danced with delight, the inevitable question was raised.

"What are you going to name the kitten, Sam?"

He wrinkled his brow in deep four-year-old concentration. The name needed to be special, not just a predictable cat name. The kitten needed a name that would remind Sam of this special birthday. And, of course, it had to be a name everyone would easily remember.

Looking in all directions for inspiration, Sam suddenly spied a stack of wood Brian had split for their campfire. He flashed a huge dimpled grin.

"Firewood!" he shouted.

"Firewood? What are you talking about?" Brian asked.

"I'm talking about my kitten," Sam replied matter-of-factly. "I'm going to name her Firewood."

Brian and Lynn looked at each other with amusement. You know what they were thinking, of course: *"Firewood? What a crazy name! You will not name your cat Firewood."*

Though they may have thought Firewood was a crazy name for a cat, they never said it. Sam is lucky to have great parents who decided that their son could name his kitten anything he wanted. And who is to say that Firewood is not an absolutely magnificent name for a cat, anyway? It is definitely not an ordinary cat name and it will forever remind Sam of his fourth birthday and the camping trip he shared with his mom and dad.

From that day forward, a cat named Firewood was part of the Stinson household. Sam and Firewood wrestled together, watched television together, even slept together. Sometimes they would play outside until almost dark and Sam could hardly see the solid black cat with the white spot on her nose.

But when it was time to go inside for a good night's sleep, Sam would call his cat by name.

"Firewood! Firewood! Time to go inside."

And no matter where she was in the neighborhood, the little black fur ball with the white spot on her nose ran swiftly to her four-year-old Master. Scooping Firewood into his arms, Sam took her inside to rest for the night.

Sam never thought Firewood was a silly name for a cat. I like to think that Firewood was quite proud of her name. She was Firewood, Sam Stinson's kitten. And Firewood was always happiest when she heard her Master calling her by name.

> *. . . The sheep hear his voice:*
> *and He calleth*
> *His own sheep by name,*
> *and leadeth them out.*
>
> *John 10:3-4*

#2.   A Dog Named Cool-Whip

"Alright," his mother relented. "You can keep a puppy. But just one."

A litter of seven small puppies nuzzled next to their mother, Duchess, a registered gold and white collie. Duchess had been bred so that the family would benefit from the extra money the puppies would bring. Eleven-year-old Ryan protested as soon as he saw the newborn creatures.

"You can't sell them! You just can't," he protested.

Even though they would go to good homes, it would indeed be hard to let each puppy go. Ryan was close to tears and his mother's heart softened. Finally, she agreed to let him keep one of the puppies as his very own. Kneeling next to Duchess, he cupped one of the small animals in his hands. Duchess allowed him to hold each one until he decided which he would keep.

"This is the one," he told his mother while holding a fine male with the beautiful coloring of his mother. His mother agreed that this puppy would not be sold and would belong to Ryan.

"What about a name?" she asked.

Without hesitation, Ryan replied, "Cool-Whip. I am going to call him Cool-Whip!"

A smile on her lips, his mother had to ask the obvious question: "Why would you name a dog Cool-Whip?"

"Because," Ryan answered calmly, "I've always wanted a dog that had his name on his bowl!"

> *. . . I will wait on thy name*
> *for it is good before thy saints.*
>
> *Psalm 52:9*

3. The Second Avenue Girl's Club

*M*y paternal grandmother is one of my heroes. Born in the late 1800s, her life was filled with love, faith, hard work, and the changing face of America during a time of incredible growth.

I was only eight months old when my grandfather died. While I do not know all the details of their life together, I do know they married when my grandfather lived in the vicinity of Walhalla, South Carolina. (Now there's a name in itself!) After marrying, my grandfather purchased land in Newnan, Georgia, and moved the entire family – wife, children, furniture, household goods, farm animals, and any other items of importance – by train. He packed everything he owned in boxcars for the move to Georgia. Settling just outside Newnan, my grandparents build a farmhouse on some of the most beautiful land in the country. It was here that my grandfather lived until his death in 1957.

Following the death of my grandfather, my grandmother remained in the farmhouse for a while. However, she later moved to Second Avenue in the city of Newnan. She lived in her white frame house until age 91, when a stroke left her unable to care for herself. She spent the remaining months of her life in a nursing home – a place she never wanted to be, but a move that was necessary for the care she required.

Though she was *Nanny* to me, her real name was Blois Stamps Lee.

Blois. Have you ever heard of such a name? I have never known anyone else with that name. It was a one-of-a-kind name for a one-of-a-kind lady!

I have often wondered why her parents gave my grandmother that name. Was it an old family name? Was she named for a family friend? Was this a common name when she was born? Did anyone make jokes about her name and did she have a hard time learning to spell it in school? I never asked her any of these questions. I wish I had.

Regardless of the answers, Blois was her name -- and she did justice to her very unusual name. When I hear her name, I picture a woman of integrity, compassion, fairness, and incredible generosity. When I hear her name, I recall colorful flowers in the front yard and a well-tended vegetable garden in the back yard. She tended both until she was ninety-one. When I hear her name, I remember colorful scraps of material piled high on her bed that became quilts for her children, grandchildren, and great grandchildren. When I hear her name, I remember fresh yeast rolls rising by the furnace and creamy divinity candy at Christmas. When I hear her name, I recall strong arms that hugged me and her sweet voice that never failed to say, "I love you."

Yet, when I hear her name, I am also thankful I was named for her sister! And I am thankful her sister's name was Annie. My middle name is Anne. I suppose I could handle being named *Cathy Blois*, but I certainly prefer *Cathy Anne*!

During her years in the house on Second Avenue, my grandmother had three special friends with unusual names of their own -- Ola, Ula, and Albertine. (Anyone want to make a wager that Albertine's father was named, maybe, Albert?)

Whatever their names, I refer to them as the "Second Avenue Girl's Club" because, until their deaths, Blois, Ola, Ula, and Albertine, watched out for one another, talked to each other every day, shopped together, shared vegetables and flowers from their gardens, gossiped a little, and laughed a lot. They were girlfriends! Trust me – I am fortunate enough to have several "girlfriends" (sisters, actually) and this is what girlfriends do! The names of my girlfriends, though, are certainly less colorful -- Deborah, Jennifer, Mary, Glenda, Janice, Caroline, Lauren, and other ordinary names. Not one Blois, Ula, Ola, or Albertine in the bunch!

Each of these women – like the men who are special friends of mine – do justice to their everyday, average, run-of-the-mill names. You see, it is not the name that makes the person – it is the person who makes the name.

Blois would not be my first choice for a name. But, Blois was a good name because of who my grandmother was and the meaning she gave to her name. I can only pray that I can do the same justice to my name that Blois, my Nanny, did with hers.

The same goes for the other members of the Second Avenue Girl's Club -- Ola, Ula, and Albertine.

Blois! It was a very good name.

*A good name
is rather to be chosen
than great riches.*

Proverbs 22:1

#4. The Voice on the Radio

When I first heard the song on the radio, I immediately knew it was Doug. Though I had not heard him sing for years, the voice was unmistakable. Jerry and I were in his room at St. Joseph's Hospital where he awaited a heart transplant. The radio played quietly in the background.

"Jer, listen!" I exclaimed. "That is Doug – I know it is. It sounds just like him."

Doug Brooks and I met when we attended Madras School together. He lived with his brother and father on Happy Valley Circle, not far from the hustle and bustle of downtown Madras, Georgia. Actually, the only hustle and bustle in Madras took place on Friday evenings when the Madras Mohawks took on surrounding schools in some serious games of basketball.

But, I digress!

Doug had a great musical talent. He could play anything at all on the guitar and he was equally talented as a singer. We used to sing and harmonize together. And I remember one special occasion when, with two other classmates, we entered and won first place in a local talent show. We sang two songs – *All I Have to do is Dream* by the Everly Brothers and *Jean*, the title song from the movie, The Prime of Miss Jean Brodie -- with Doug playing the guitar on both. This was the sixties and we needed an appropriate name, of course. We finally called ourselves "The Liquid Spirit," a name we spotted on the side of bottle of mimeograph fluid. Remember the purple mimeograph machines you cranked by hand? Lord, I am getting old!

86

But, I digress!

Doug always said he intended to be one of two things – a country music singer or a mechanic. And, years later on a Saturday afternoon at St. Joseph's Hospital, I realized that his dream of being a country music singer had prevailed. The voice that sang "I'd be better off in a pine box on a slow train back to Georgia. . ." was definitely that of my friend, Doug Brooks.

Except now he was Doug Stone. Whatever the last name, I knew that voice. I celebrated for him and longed to see him just to say how proud I was that he had recognized his dream. I told my friends and urged them to buy his records to support him in his music.

Doug was scheduled to appear a couple of years later at "Concerts in the Country" near Lake Lanier in Georgia. My friend, Jim, offered me tickets.

"You say he is a friend of yours," Jim said with a grin. "Why don't you go see him? I can't make it that night so here are two tickets."

Did Jim doubt that I actually knew Doug? I don't know. But I took the tickets and invited my friend, Mimi, to go along with me.

"You know Doug Stone?" she asked with an air of skepticism.

"Yes," I said impatiently. "Why doesn't anyone believe me?"

On the night of the concert Mimi and I took our seats on the seventh row. She continued to stare at me cynically. Sherry and John, friends who joined us, also looked at me with questioning eyes. For a few moments I even questioned myself – did I really know Doug or did my brain have the hiccups?

The answer came about thirty minutes after Doug took the stage. Of course, the concert hall was filled with thousands of screaming fans who were clapping and singing along with familiar songs. They clapped the loudest, though, when it was announced that those who wished could come in a line to the front of the stage for close-up photos. This is a tradition at "Concerts in the Country" and the fans enjoy the chance to snap photos at close range.

Well, I had my camera and I was on a mission. Waiting for the right moment, I moved to the very end of the line. I walked the seven rows to the base of the stage and held the camera before my face. After snapping a couple of photos, I was returning to my seat when I heard a familiar voice say, "Hi, Cathy! It's good to see you!"

The familiar voice was that of my friend, Doug, who had stopped singing when he recognized me after, lo, these many years. Not only that, he paused long enough to call me my name. Boy, was I relieved. I waved as I returned to my seat with a very smug look on my face. I said nothing as I quietly took my seat. But let me tell you that Mimi, Sherry, and John glanced at me with a different look on their faces.

Doug ended the song he was singing and, to my surprise, spoke to the audience.

"I'm so glad to see my friend Cathy Lee here tonight," he said, not knowing my last name had changed to Phillips when I married.

He continued, "Cathy and I used to sing together. We went to school together and even went to parties together. She taught me a lot . . ."

Of course, the audience whooped and hollered at that comment. Raising one eyebrow, I could not help but give my friends an "I told you I knew him" look.

They were impressed. I was smug.

I recognized the voice and Doug recognized me and spoke to me in front of thousands of strangers – and three skeptical friends.

He called me by name. What a relief!

Peace be to you.
Our friends salute thee.
Greet the friends there
by name.

III John 1:14

#5. That's Cathy with a "C"

$\mathcal{A}$ brilliant basketball career was cut short because of a typographical error in the newspaper. I'm convinced of it.

Picture it. The final night of the county basketball tournament was being held at the Madras School gymnasium. The Madras Mohawks were vying for the first place trophy against the girl's team from Moreland School. I was a part of that Madras team – not a really important part – but, along with everyone else, I wanted that trophy.

As we huddled together that night, the gym was electric with the excitement of the players, parents, and other fans. Each of our games with Moreland that season had been very close, so the tension mounted as the clocked ticked off the minutes until the first jump-ball began the game.

The Madras Mohawks gained first possession of ball. Connie Coggin, her blond ponytail flying, made a fast break for the goal. Two points. I clapped and yelled from my spot on the bench. Connie and I had been friends practically since birth. We attended the same school and the same church. Connie's mother, Margaret, sat beside my mother in the stands. They were cheering in stereo for Connie. Margaret was like another mother to me and I knew she would cheer just as loudly if I scored.

The scored bounced back and forth by only two points for the first quarter. Each time we scored, one of the Moreland girls answered our effort with two points for their team. It was going to be a long night.

Suddenly, the coach called my name. I trembled! I wanted to play but I didn't want to play. Do you know the feeling? I was to go in and take a couple of long shots. While I wanted to be a part of the win, what if I made some tragic mistake that cost us the game? I felt the pressure.

The coach instructed me to go in and take a couple of long shots. My short stature usually prevented me from getting beneath the goal. So I practiced shots I could take a good distance away from the goal. I became pretty good at those outside shots. But the truth was that I seemed to only be good for a mere six points per game.

Six points. That seemed to be my limit. Really, the first three times I touched the ball I could throw it from practically any position on the court and it would slice through the basket with a hallelujah swish! Whether it was a lay-up shot or an outside shot from right court, the ball was in the hoop. . . but only three times. After my six points, I usually could shoot all night and never place the ball in the vicinity of that goal again. Six-point Cathy. Connie Coggin, on the other hand, was more of a fourteen-point girl. Well, if I had six points in me, I was more than happy to add them to our score.

Cathy Lee, #5, entered the game.

True to my reputation, I shot and hit two baskets from strange positions on the court. I kept thinking that I only had one more shot in me before being benched for good. As my thoughts wandered, my hands suddenly held the basketball. Connie passed it to me as we were all charging down the court. I was in the clear and in the perfect position for a lay-up shot. I ran, dribbling the ball while calculating the proper location at which I would jump and, with luck, place that ball softly into the hoop.

Just then I saw a flash from the corner of my eye. A photographer from the local newspaper was standing at the end of the court, just inches from me. To this day, I cannot remember whether the ball went into the basket or not. I simply know that a bright flashed killed my concentration. In its place came dreams of the star I would most certainly become as a result of this publicity. Regardless of the countless photos snapped that night, I was certain that mine would be in the county newspaper, thus beginning a brilliant basketball career.

I am happy to report that the Madras Mohawks went on to win the first-place trophy by three points. However, it all seemed a bit anticlimactic compared to the media hype that would surely surround me when the paper hit the stands on Thursday.

Almost a full week crawled by before the Thursday paper was published. My mother held a copy in her hand as I got off the bus that afternoon. Her smile was obvious confirmation that my photo was sitting inside the sports section. I dropped my books on the table and quickly grabbed the page she folded back. There I was – Madras Mohawk #5. The paper had the full story of the nail-biting game. Then, beneath my photo, they even had a caption: *Driving toward the goal in tournament play for Madras School is #5, Kathy Lee.*

Kathy? KATHY?

That was not my name. My name is Cathy . . . with a "C." My name does not have a "K" in it. The picture was me, but the name did not belong to me. I dropped the paper on the dining room table and went to my room where my dreams of a brilliant basketball career vanished. How would the scouts ever find me? They would be searching for someone whose name began with a "K." My dream was gone before it even began. I was so frustrated that I could not even get excited about my picture being in the paper. My thoughts centered on the incorrect spelling of my name. They would never have spelled Connie Coggin's name with a "K."

I am Cathy . . . with a "C." Get it right, okay?

●●●●●

Quite a few years have passed since I played basketball at Madras School. Not one basketball scout has visited or even called during that time. Could it be the fault of one simple typographical error? Was it because I was only good for six points per game? Was it because the Women's National Basketball Association did not exist then? Or was it simply that I was meant to do other things? Whatever the reason, I still am frustrated when people misspell my name – Kathy, Cathie, Kathi, etc. Whatever the spelling, mine was, is, and will forever be Cathy with a "C."

I could never have envisioned all that life held for me when I was a Madras Mohawk. Life was simple – a small town circling an old Courthouse, a tightly knit school and community, a home on the farm, and a church service at 11:00 every Sunday. It seemed those things were enough to fill up life pretty well in the 1960s.

Things are not so simple any longer. Instead of living in the same small town, I have moved many times – especially when I was a United Methodist Minister's wife. I occasionally visit the town where I grew up, but Newnan is no longer small nor does it simply circle the old Courthouse. It spills out into places that were pastures and woods when I was growing up. Instead of a tightly knit community, I live in a subdivision where we come and go so quickly we wave but never really learn the names of our neighbors.

My life has changed dramatically since I occupied a farmhouse on Posey Road. I have been to college and graduate school, held a variety of jobs, and met more people than I could possibly remember. My world has grown larger than the familiar creeks and meadows of a farm just outside Newnan. I have walked the beaches of Cancun and played the slot machines in Las Vegas. I have climbed pyramids in Mexico and glaciers in Alaska. I have flown in huge planes to business meetings and vacations and I have seen snow-covered mountain peaks by helicopter. I have endured a nerve-wracking crossing of Lake

Pontchartrain by railway and have cruised to beautiful ports of call on luxury ships. I have watched the Space Shuttle lift off in Florida and have played aboard the Shuttle trainer in NASA in Houston.

I have made wonderful friends who support me in my dreams and endeavors, my joys and sorrows. I have lost people who did not understand my motives or give me the benefit of the doubt. I have loved people and lost them either to time or death. I have loved people who will always be with me in body or in spirit.

I have worked in churches and businesses and learned many lessons along the way. I have written books and articles that have blessed people and, in turn, blessed me. I have been humbled at the ways in which God has used me to help others and I have been humbled at the many blessings He has provided me.

I have loved a man with all my heart and have experienced his unconditional love in return. I have memories of a huge spring wedding and a home we built together. And I have memories of hospital rooms, a heart transplant, an emergency phone call giving me the worst news of my life, and sitting beside an open grave on a cold January day. I have experienced the pain of grief, depression, and the desire to completely give up. And I have experienced the rebirth of joy and laughter in my life.

In short, there are days when I barely recognize that #5 Madras Mohawk from so many years ago. There have been so many experiences and so many changes that, quite often, I feel that the only thing that remains constant is my name . . . that's Cathy with a "C."

I was Cathy then and I am Cathy now. Everything else seems to have changed far more than I ever could have imagined. As with all of us, some changes have been good while others have been quite painful. We are born into a world with no idea of what that it holds for each of us.

The first gift we are given, though, is a name.

The name given to me was Cathy . . . with a "C." It has served me well and it has been the one constant in my life.

When someone knows me by name, they do not simply know *about* me, they really *know* me – the things that make me laugh as well as the things that make me hurt; the questions I ask as well as the answers I have discovered. When someone knows me by name they take the time to learn all the events and experiences that make up who I am. When someone knows me by name, there is a certain kinship and familiarity that abides.

"Be at peace," Jerry used to say to me quite often. And I can be at peace because, whatever change may come, my name remains the same – that's Cathy with a "C."

God knows me. He knows me by name.

Be at peace. That is enough.

Fear not for I have redeemed thee;
I have called thee by name;
thou art mine.
When thou passest through the waters,
I will be with thee:
and through the rivers,
they shall not overflow thee:
when thou walkest through the fire,
thou shalt not be burned;
neither shall the flame kindle upon thee.
For I am the Lord, thy God,
the Holy One of Israel, thy Savior.

Isaiah 43: 1-3

Welcome, blessed spring!

Winter's lessons have been learned.

Blossom – stand your ground!

Fried Green Tomato Theology

Summer brought good news and bad news to Posey Road.

The bad news? It was time to plant and work in the garden and I hated to work in the garden.

The good news? That garden produced fried green tomatoes and, you guessed it, I love fried green tomatoes. With ketchup.

My mother had a wonderful way with those tomatoes. Gently picking only the tender, medium-sized tomatoes, she washed them thoroughly and placed them on an old wooden cutting board. Using her favorite stainless steel knife, she sliced and discarded the ends of each tomato before carefully cutting the young pale-green spheres into thin round pieces for frying. A touch of salt and pepper flavored each side before they were dusted with a coating of corn meal and a dash of flour. A familiar black cast iron skillet was brought from its hiding place beneath the kitchen counter and, in short order, green tomatoes were sizzling on the front eye of the stove. Once they were an appropriate golden brown, Mama placed them on a white oval plate that went immediately to the table. Sitting in the middle of the oak table, the aroma of those fried green tomatoes called us all to supper. Within just a few minutes, those very same fried green tomatoes were sitting inside our happy stomachs. Mine, with ketchup.

Getting those fried green tomatoes to the table, though, involved a long process of plowing, laying off rows, and purchasing the best tomato plants available. With that job behind us, the time for planting arrived.

In addition to my father, there were four main players in the fried green tomato game. Because we had a large tract of land, we shared garden space with other families on Posey Road. In return, assorted members of these families would help plant, hoe, weed, pick, shell, etc., the various edibles that grew in this quiet corner of our property. From these various Posey Road residents, my father hand-picked four of us specifically for the task of planting tomatoes according to a system he developed and required that we follow to the last precise detail.

The youngest participant, Little Doodlebug, belonged to the Richardson family that lived at the entrance to Posey Road. Little Doodlebug, so named because his father was known as Big Doodlebug, dropped individual tomato plants along the row at specific intervals based on Daddy's instructions. Next in line was Little Doodlebug's sister, Arlene, who dug a hole in the soft brown dirt next to each tomato plant. The third process involved Raylinda Dupree, my cousin twice-removed on my Mama's side and the scourge of my childhood who, much to my frustration, was a semi-permanent resident at our house. Fussing all the way, Raylinda carried a water bucket with a big metal ladle. She poured enough water into the hole to create a wonderfully dirty, smelly, soupy mud that crept beneath your fingernails and left long-lasting stains on your hands. I know this from personal experience because, being the oldest, my job was the final step in the process. I actually set the tomato plants in the aforementioned dirty, smelly, soupy mud. I grew increasingly filthy as I slid along each row on my backside, scooping up this black, gooey mixture of dirt and water, then heaping it around each tomato plant. Daddy was a fierce taskmaster who demanded that all plants be standing straight and tall in each row before my job was complete.

I hated my job. I hated the mud beneath my fingernails and my rough, dirty hands. I wanted one of the easier jobs such as dropping plants or pouring water. But my task was based on my age, ability, and the direction of my father. Though I complained, whined, and developed a generally obnoxious attitude, my job remained the same. Regardless of my pouting, my work was a critical element in getting those fried green tomatoes to the table.

Teamwork was the secret to our success. Even though my assignment seemed the most demanding in my eyes, it was really no more important than the tasks assigned to Little Doodlebug, Arlene, and Raylinda Dupree, my cousin twice-removed on my Mama's side and the scourge of my childhood. The final participant in this assembly-line procedure was Mama herself who picked, sliced, and fried those tomatoes we all loved to eat. Mine, with ketchup.

What is Fried Green Tomato Theology, then?

Simply put, it is finding your own calling in life and doing it. It is seeing the work of each individual as equally important and necessary in the grand scheme of things. There are cardiologists and there are hairstylists. There are horse trainers and astronauts. There are actors, singers, computer technicians, teachers, rocket scientists, housewives, and househusbands. We all have a job to do.

The same is true within the church. In fact, did you know that Fried Green Tomato Theology is discussed in the Bible? Well, maybe not in the same words, but consider these verses from I Corinthians 12:

"There are diversities of gifts, but the same Spirit. There are differences of service, but the same Lord. There are diversities of operations, but the same God works all of them . . . For as the body is one, and hath many members, and all the members of that one body, being many, are one body: so also is Christ. . . But now hath God set the members every one of them in the body, as it hath pleased Him. . . The eye cannot say unto the hand, I have no need of thee: nor again the head to the feet, I have no need of you. . . there should be no division in the body; but that the members should have the same care one for another. And whether one member suffer, all the members suffer with it; or one member be honored, all the members rejoice with it. Now ye are the body of Christ, and members in particular."

What spiritual lessons can be learned from a simple plate of fried green tomatoes? Consider these things. We each have certain gifts from God. There are nursery workers and there are youth leaders. There are Sunday School teachers and there are janitors. There are preachers, educators, ushers, and secretaries.

So then, whether my gift is planting a fine row of tomatoes or leading a church retreat, it is my responsibility to accept, develop, and use my Spiritual Gift. We must respect and encourage others in their own ministry. We must recognize that, though others may have different responsibilities, all ministry is equally important and necessary in the eyes of God. Finally, we must listen carefully to our Heavenly Father who calls us and equips us to work according to His direction.

I still love fried green tomatoes. With ketchup. And every few years I plant a handful of tomatoes so that I can pick them when they are pale-green and tender. I slice them, sprinkle them with a bit of salt and pepper, and use the familiar dusting of corn meal and a dash of flour. I now own the old black cast-iron skillet that can still fry a green tomato to golden perfection!

Now, though, whenever I munch fried green tomatoes with ketchup I realize the lessons I learned in a garden on Posey Road so many years ago. Those lessons go much deeper than simply growing juicy tomatoes. At stake is recognizing our God-given gifts. At stake is recognizing and respecting the gifts given to others. At stake is working together to build the Kingdom of God – on earth as it is in heaven.

I thank God that the lessons learned many years ago in a garden on Posey Road remind me to be about my Father's business and to do it with all my heart to the glory of God.

How sweet it is!

Now
concerning spiritual gifts,
brethren,
I would not have you
ignorant.

I Corinthians 12:1

Cathy Lee Phillips

Cathy Lee Phillips

Oh, Do You Know The Cake Lady?

> *Blossom and Stand Your Ground!*

$\mathcal{E}$ ach week, an ordinary sedan turned into the parking lot of Orange United Methodist Church. The occupant might arrive on a rainy Tuesday morning or in the summer sun of a Thursday afternoon. Perhaps she slipped by unnoticed as daylight was fading. She quickly emerged from her car with a tightly-wrapped package held firmly in her hands. Because my office faced the front of the building, I usually saw her first. Leaving my desk, I walked the few steps to the office of Mary Johnson, ace Church Secretary and one of my favorite adopted sisters.

"It's here," I announce.

Mary opened the door and we received the package. We simply smiled as she disappeared into the mist.

The Cake Lady of Orange had come and gone.

The package was the same each week -- her specialty -- a luscious to-die-for pound cake loaded with calories, gooey fat grams, and a heaping portion of love. Fresh from her kitchen, the cake was usually still warm with an aroma so sweet, I believe that simply sniffing it would automatically add five pounds to the hips.

Fighting the temptation to devour the cake ourselves (and never tell a soul), Mary and I quickly decided who would receive the Cake of the Week. The decision was never difficult because the Cake Lady had timing that was downright eerie and/or miraculous. Her cake inevitably appeared whenever someone was grieving, celebrating, ailing, or just generally stove up. Within minutes of its delivery to the church office, the Cake of the Week was on its way to the lucky recipient(s).

The Cake Lady was quite a tradition at Orange United Methodist Church when Mary and I were staff members there. The Cake Lady continued her ministry on one unyielding condition -- that she remained anonymous. Along with certain members of her family, only Mary and I knew her identity. And we will never tell! Certificates, accolades, or special recognition did not motivate the Cake Lady. She simply ministered in the way God called and equipped her. While her anonymity was part of the mystery and the fun, it was also an important part of her mission.

Quiet and unassuming, the Cake Lady was amazed and bemused by the fuss she caused. Though famous in the church and community, she still sat and walked among us as any other mortal. Nevertheless, she was discussed at church meetings. Choir members tried to guess her identity. Sunday School Classes speculated on her secret recipe. Several cases of "cake envy" were even reported and, if you listened closely, you would often hear certain members bragging, "Yes, we have received *The Cake* – have you?"

The woman even received fan mail at the church office!

So, if not recognition, what was her motivation?

In her words, "Some people preach, some teach, and some sing in the choir. This is what I can do."

The Cake Lady of Orange was never elected by a Charge Conference or voted on by the Administrative Council. Her position was not posted in the United Methodist Church Discipline nor was it funded by any group within the church.

Nevertheless, her ministry was as vital as that of any group or individual.

Our world could use a few more Cake Ladies, I believe. Those who use their various gifts in ministry and do not care who receives the credit; those who quietly seek to do what they can for the glory of God; those who understand God does not limit ministry simply to those who have gone through a process of ordination, certification, or official recognition.

Who knows? Maybe more Cake Ladies will come forward.

And if your church is lucky enough to have one, let me say to her, "You go, girl! Thank you for your quiet ministry. And save me a piece of chocolate cake, would you?"

*And whatsoever ye do
in word or deed,
do all in the name of the Lord Jesus,
giving thanks to God and the Father
through him.*

Colossians 3:17

Cathy Lee Phillips

Literal Lydia

> **Blossom and Stand Your Ground**

*The Biggs family are active members of
Johns Creek United Methodist Church just north of Atlanta,
where they serve, grow in faith, and worship
with my friend, Dr. Dee Shelnutt.*

*L*ydia Biggs awoke that April morning determined to be the best Purple Dolphin ever.

"Mom, they named the soccer team after me!" she exclaimed to my good friend, Lauren. I met Lauren in 1990 when she was a nurse at St. Joseph's Hospital and part of the team evaluating my husband, Jerry, for a new heart. In the midst of my terror, Lauren's warm smile and compassion lessened my fear. We have been friends since that frightening day, long before there was seven-year-old Lydia, three-year-old Georgianna, and little Alyssa Lauren, a beautiful eight-pound bundle who entered the world on August 16, 2001.

"They named the team after you?" Lauren inquired.

"Well, my name is Lydia and in the Bible she was a seller of purple and my team is the Purple Dolphins," she reasoned.

It's hard to argue with logic like that. It is even harder to argue with a seven-year-old, so Lauren just smiled silently.

"Is Daddy coming to the game?" she asked for the third time.

"Yes, Honey. He wouldn't miss it."

Lauren was amazed at how the Purple Dolphins had transformed her mild-mannered husband into a wild soccer fan. Calm and relaxed, David preferred the quiet serenity of a golf course to the loud roar of team sports – that is, until Lydia became a Purple Dolphin. Suddenly David, clad in a matching purple jersey, was on the sidelines running up and down the field with the team, transformed into a bona fide soccer dad.

When game time approached, Lydia brushed her blonde-brown hair into a tight ponytail. She donned her uniform and her hazel-blue-green eyes danced with anticipation. Grabbing a purple water bottle from the kitchen, she jumped into the car and bounced happily in the seat.

As they backed out of the driveway, Lydia suddenly shrieked, "Wait! I forgot something!"

She ran into the house. Lauren, David, Georgianna, and Alyssa, waited . . . and waited . . . and waited.

"Do you think she got scared and decided not to play?" they wondered.

Lauren walked inside and climbed the stairs to Lydia's room. Following a strange jingling noise, she found Lydia sitting on the floor of her room shaking her black and white cow-patterned piggy bank. A few pennies lay on the floor near her.

"What are you doing, honey?" Lauren asked, completely puzzled.

"I need more money, Mom."

"Why do you need money for your soccer game, Lydia?"

And Lydia, the literal, the logical, responded with seven-year-old earnestness.

"Because the coach said we could sit out for a quarter!"

Ah, the simplicity of a child! Between chuckles, Lauren explained the difference between a quarter (25 cents) and a quarter (period of play in a soccer game).

Lydia learned something that day and, as so often happens, so did the rest of us. My life would be so easier if I trusted my Savior as much as Lydia trusted her coach – a Savior who tells me, "Come to me if you are weary and burdened and I will give you rest." When I am tired and used up, I can sit out for a quarter, catch my breath, garner new strength, and Christ will carry my load. Though I hear these familiar words, my adult mind often gets in the way. And while Lydia has certainty, I have doubt. While Lydia accepts, I question. While Lydia listens with sincerity, I listen with skepticism.

She is beautiful and clever and witty. And, yes, I have laughed about her frantic search for money so that she "could sit out for a quarter."

After all, that is what the coach said and Lydia literally believed her.

Lydia Biggs, a fine United Methodist named for the seller of purple, believes the words of her coach and, more importantly, sincerely believes the words of her Savior.

And, once more, I learn about Christ through the wisdom of a child.

Literally.

> *Whosoever therefore
> shall humble himself as this little child,
> the same is greatest
> in the kingdom of heaven.*
>
> *Matthew 18:4*

Girlfriend Day '95

┌─────────────────────────────────────┐
│ *Blossom and Stand Your Ground* │
└─────────────────────────────────────┘

The Date: **April 5, 1995**
The Players: **Jennifer Huycke, my best buddy, and me**
The Event: **Girlfriend Day '95**

*S*o I suppose you are wondering, "What is Girlfriend Day?"

Simply stated, it is an annual outing celebrating friendship. Of course, I realize that most people spend special time with friends, but Girlfriend Day is unique and characterized by certain essential elements.

First, you obviously need a friend. Jennifer Huycke is my choice for this annual outing. Next, you need a day with no other obligations (good luck finding this!).

Once these basic requirements have been met, the fun begins – shopping, lunching, laughing, and talking. You know, girlfriend things. Oh, and I almost forgot . . . chocolate! I do realize, of course, that men would probably prefer something along the lines of fishing, golfing, and beef jerky. Our version of Girlfriend Day certainly does not include beef jerky – only the girl things mentioned above.

Without a doubt, Girlfriend Day '95 has been the most memorable so far for Jennifer and me. It began harmlessly enough. Jennifer and I spent the morning in the mall where the shopping was plentiful -- and so was the chocolate. We lunched at Olive Garden then wandered among the shops across the street from the mall.

Though we are best friends, Jennifer and I have very different tastes in clothing.   I like beautiful floral designs. Jennifer likes weird geometric shapes. I prefer soothing pink and blue pastels. Jennifer goes for bright primary colors. Though we might enter a store together, we quickly go to our separate corners and the game begins. We grab sweaters, pants, shirts, and dresses. We grab almost anything off the "For Sale" rack. And if a "Clearance" sign is anywhere within the store, it's a feeding frenzy. To be honest, Jennifer has been known to chase flashing blue lights from one corner of K-Mart to the other. In fact, the blue light on a passing police car causes her body to immediate secrete large quantities of shopping hormones.

Very little conversation is required during the Girlfriend Day shopping free-for-all.   Therefore, store employees rarely know we are shopping together, let alone celebrating an annual event.

In one store, however, Jennifer asked my opinion regarding a sweater she found. It was beautiful – not at all what I expected her to select. The background was a soft ivory and it was adorned with petite flowers and designs embroidered in pale pinks and greens. The good news was that it was on sale. The bad news was that it was missing one of the pearl buttons that adorned the front of the sweater. The missing button was in a very obvious place and was so unique we knew the odds of finding a match were not good.

"Maybe they have a spare button," I suggested.

"Or maybe they will give me another $10 off the price," Jennifer responded. (Yes, she is my best friend but, quite frankly, Jennifer can be really cheap at times).

We walked to the cashier, each holding a pile of clothing to purchase. Jennifer, of course, was quick to mention the missing button. From beneath the counter the cashier pulled a box containing buttons of every size, shape, and color imaginable. Alas, no match was to be found.

Smelling blood, Jennifer moved in for the kill.

"Well, is it possible to have the sweater at a reduced price since we cannot find a matching button?" Jennifer asked so sweetly.

The cashier was obviously going to grant her request. It was then that, I suppose, the devil just grabbed hold of me.

"Excuse me, ma'am," I spoke to the cashier in my most self-righteous voice, "but I cannot remain silent. (Can you feel the drama?) I must tell you that I just saw this woman rip the button off that sweater."

Dead silence.

Not realizing we were actually friends celebrating Girlfriend Day '95, the cashier stuttered and stammered, obviously not knowing what to do or say. After a moment, however, Jennifer became quite vocal.

"You lie!" she suddenly shrieked, her eyes wide with surprise. "You must die!"

Sweat popped out on the brow of the cashier. She must have feared a rumble right there in the middle of Fashion Bug.

"I'm sorry," I replied innocently, "but I've never seen this woman before in my life."

By this time I was becoming concerned about Jennifer's red face and blood pressure. Her shock quickly turned to laughter and our nervous cashier finally realized this was an innocent joke between two good friends. This innocent cashier even laughed with us. All three of us held our sides as tears ran down our faces. We explained our annual outing to the frazzled cashier who thought Girlfriend Day was a grand idea.

We all decided that moment would obviously be the highlight of Girlfriend Day '95.

The button was never found. Jennifer did buy her sweater at a $10 reduced price. The cashier was still laughing as we left. And I'll never forget her parting words.

"A friendship like yours is a real blessing from heaven!"

Yes ma'am, it is. It really is."

Two are better than one;
because they have a good reward
for their labor.
For if they fall,
the one will lift up his fellow:
but woe to him
that is alone when he falleth;
for he hath not another
to help him up.

Ecclesiastes 4:9-10

Not A Bad Day At All!

*R*aylinda Dupree was mean – notoriously mean. Her evil nature was legendary in our corner of the county. The scourge of my childhood, Raylinda came to live with us after her parents divorced.

"Just eat up with meanness!" adults and children alike often observed. Raylinda's hobbies included gossip, insults, and bodily harm to anyone who kept her from getting her way in all situations. She regularly invented elaborate tales about other Posey Road residents -- me included. Then, she smiled proudly as she sat back and watched the trouble that ensued.

"That girl could make a nun cuss," said Mr. Wright who lived at the end of Posey Road. I doubt Mr. Wright ever met a nun personally but, knowing Raylinda, I was willing to take his word for it.

Thinking they would just be fighting a losing battle, no one ever tried to tame Raylinda's meanness. That made living with her all the more wearisome. Raylinda could quickly infuriate even the most kind-hearted adult. She was in constant danger of being punched by children of all ages – at home on Posey Road, at school, even at church. I usually wanted to punch her myself. But she was kin, my cousin twice-removed on my

Mama's side, so I couldn't punch her. To make matters worse, I was supposed to keep the other kids from punching her, too. I was the oldest and Posey Road law decreed that an older relative had to safeguard a younger one – like it or not. For the record, I did not like it at all.

Then there was one final factor that made the situation almost intolerable.

Raylinda was thin.

"That girl is mean as a rattlesnake with hemorrhoids but doesn't she have a cute figure?" people muttered.

I, on the other hand, was a chubby child. I preferred *chubby*. Raylinda, however, delighted in referring to me as *barrel-shaped*, or *big as a horse* or *just plain fat*.

"Just ignore what she says," Mama lectured. "After all, she is kinfolk and you are the oldest."

Raylinda's tongue, though, never took a rest. Despite her constant barrage of non-endearing terms, she expected my protection when, inevitably, she had someone ready to punch her. Raylinda was indeed an unwelcome burden. Yet I was honor-bound to protect her. And, speaking fairly, she really did have a cute figure.

Life's unfairness weighed heavily on me one hot August evening in '69. Raylinda was especially burdensome during the summer months when there was no school as a diversion from her wicked ways. My life was filled with her insults from daybreak until bedtime. I was stuck with her for hours as she continually taunted and insulted me. Yet I endured. I was the oldest, you see.

Nevertheless, on this particular day, Raylinda's words, merely irritating at first, turned maddening as the day progressed. As the temperature rose, so did my anger. Finally, while we worked in the garden just before dark, my fury approached explosive proportions. Supper was over and Raylinda was happily reminding me that I had eaten two biscuits while she had eaten only one.

"You'll never have a figure like mine," she ridiculed me yet again.

"Ignore her," I said to myself as I hoed the butter beans.

"My clothes are much prettier than yours because I can wear any style," Raylinda bragged.

"Remember that she could make a nun cuss," I reminded myself as I picked the okra.

"Your Mama says she has to order your clothes from the Chubby section of the Sears catalog. I think chubby is only a nice word for being just plain fat."

"It is better to eat two biscuits than to be as mean as a rattlesnake with hemorrhoids," I pondered through clenched teeth as I watered the tomatoes.

"You'll probably be an old maid but, with my figure, I'll more than likely marry a doctor or lawyer and live in that new subdivision on Smokey Road," she boasted.

Enough!

I was hot. I was tired. I was sick of her meanness and her cute figure. And, if the truth were known, I had my own dream of one day living in a big brick house in that new subdivision on Smokey Road.

At long last, years and years of outrage crawled to the surface on that hot August evening. Oldest or not, I reached for my wicked little cousin twice-removed on my Mama's side and threw her cute little figure into the dark dirt between the okra and the pole beans. Using the element of surprise to my advantage, I picked up a hefty, perfectly-shaped dirt clod in my right hand. I forced the clod into her face, turning and twisting it until nothing remained but a few stray pieces of rich Georgia soil. Crying vigorously, Raylinda's tears carved muddy black gullies down the front of her face.

Of course, I had read all about turning the other cheek. I knew the Bible said: "Vengeance is mine saith the Lord." At that moment, though, I somehow felt I was acting as God's agent in putting a stop to evil right there on Posey Road!

I felt so alive! So invincible! So completely vindicated! Life was good . . . for a moment.

Meanwhile, at the opposite end of the garden, Daddy glanced over his shoulder. He was unaware of the circumstances that led me to this vicious, albeit completely understandable behavior. Daddy only observed that I, the older one, was beating the devil out of Raylinda Dupree, the younger one (with the really cute figure). This was clearly a flagrant violation of Posey Road Law.

Punishment: One serious belting.

Daddy fumbled with his belt buckle as he staggered across the soft brown earth. Realizing that one good belting was imminent, I decided to obtain the greatest pleasure possible for the punishment I was about to endure. As Daddy made his way toward me, I continued the rather gratifying task at hand. All the while, however, I kept one eye on Daddy, mentally calculating the time remaining before the belt made its first contact with my bare legs.

Approaching from the left and about five feet away, Daddy made one final determined tug on his brown belt. All too late he realized he was wearing the one-size-too-large pants Aunt Ola had given him the previous Christmas. With his final yank, the belt gave way and so did his britches – falling gracefully into the rich, brown dirt, right between the okra and the pole beans.

Turning away from my evil cousin, I beheld my father – belt in his right hand and his britches crumpled around his feet. He wore only a dirty t-shirt, blue and white checkered boxers, and a shocked expression.

Dropping the remnants of the dirt clod, I did the only logical thing.

I laughed. I laughed out loud. I laughed long and hard. Even Raylinda laughed through the mud and tears. I laughed even as my legs felt the sting of the serious belting that, by now, seemed only a minor inconvenience compared to the startling event that had just transpired.

I was sent to bed early that night. Snuggling beneath my comfortable old patchwork quilt, I still felt the sting of Daddy's brown belt on my legs.

But I smiled as sleep chased me that hot August night. Beltings would come and go. But this blessed day would live in Posey Road history! I had, at least momentarily, silenced the meanest girl in the county. And I had watched my Daddy's britches drop unexpectedly into the brown Georgia dirt.

All things considered, it was not a bad day.

Not a bad day at all.

> *This is the day*
> *the Lord has made;*
> *let us rejoice and*
> *be glad in it.*
>
> *Psalm 118:24*

Cathy Lee Phillips

Just Going Through Purgatory

Blossom and Stand Your Ground

Allen was her first child and though he was approaching the age of twelve, he was still her "baby."

Those thoughts struck her as she walked through the den one Saturday evening, a load of laundry clasped between her arms and chest. She glanced at her firstborn child stretched comfortably on the floor in front of the television. Allen was an Atlanta Braves fan and his team was fighting the New York Yankees for the World Series trophy. Completely absorbed in the game, Allen was lying on his back with his arms crossed behind his head for a pillow.

Despite the clothes in her hands, his mother glanced down and, for the first time, observed tufts of small brown hair emerging from his armpit. In shock, she dropped the clothes and exclaimed in a stunned voice, "Allen! You are growing hair under your arms!" Her hands covered her mouth and she froze with an expression of alarm on her face.

Allen remained composed despite his mother's obvious trauma.

"Oh, Mom, it is no big deal," he replied calmly. I'm just going through purgatory!"

*Speaking the truth in love,
we may grow up into Him
in all things,
which is the head,
even Christ.*

Ephesians 4:15-16

The Little Puppy That Could

Blossom and Stand Your Ground

Runt of the litter, he was. With his red-brown coloring and dark eyes, he was a beautiful miniature of whatever mixture his mother was. Obviously the "love'em and leave'em" type, neither the identity nor lineage of his father was ever discovered. The tiny pup was the smallest of six born in a dark corner beneath the house on Posey Road.

The underneath of our house was quite a popular birthing place for various dogs and cats that populated Posey Road. It was cool, dark, and virtually inaccessible to humans – except for young tomboys undaunted by whatever creeping and crawling creatures shared the space. When the house became quiet at night I often listened for the unmistakable soft squeaks of newborn puppies or kittens lying next to their mother in an isolated corner beneath the house. When I heard these sounds I could hardly wait for daylight and the chance to locate the newest residents of Posey Road.

This particular autumn night, I heard the familiar squeak and before breakfast the next morning, I had crawled under the house and found a mother dog carefully guarding six newborn furry puppies. When I first saw the tiniest of the litter, he quickly

125

captured my heart. Okay, I am a sucker for the underdog, and I watched as this little one fought his way toward his mother and her abundant food supply. I also watched as his five bigger and equally hungry siblings pushed him to the back of the line. But with dogged determination, this scrappy little one fought his way back to the source of nourishment. Though he received sustenance, he remained smaller than his other four-legged siblings.

The puppies remained secluded during their first few weeks. As their eyes opened and they grew stronger, they crawled from beneath the house and explored the outside world.

This dog remained the smallest, but he was tough and strong for his size. Because of his strength and his thick furry hair, I called him Samson. I thought the name fit him well, though there were some who snickered at this small runt of a puppy sharing the name of the strong man of the Old Testament. But the puppy had gumption, stamina, resourcefulness, and yes, guts. He had learned to fend for himself and that life did not promise him any favors.

So it was that Samson became a well-known, albeit, petite member of the Posey Road citizenry. He made his place in the world and never caused a problem until the day he caught sight of the hog's head.

Dare I call it "puppy love" at first sight?

The hog's head was a by-product of butchering that had taken place earlier in the day. Several families had gathered to, delicately stated, *convey* two pigs from the pen to the freezer. This "conveyance" is hard work and usually a full day is dedicated to butchering one pig.

This group, though, felt that two pigs could be butchered, gutted, and prepared for the freezer if we began before daybreak. Thus, the process began one cold morning and by mid-afternoon, the procedure was well underway.

As mentioned previously *(Reference "A Pig Under Pressure" from <u>Silver in the Slop</u>, page 53)*, the preparation of Brunswick Stew was a regular part of the day's activity. While there are many variations on the classic Brunswick Stew recipe, ours included using meat from the hog's head as the essential ingredient of the stew. Normal procedure involved boiling the aforementioned head in a black cauldron over an open fire. When the steam began rising from the pot on a cold day, it appeared as though a smelly witches brew was a'simmering on Posey Road. The objective was to boil the head until the tender meat fell off the head, leaving behind only a few naked bones and a set of clenched teeth.

I do admit that the procedure may sound a bit gory and those of you unaccustomed to this way of life may need to pause and quickly guzzle a bottle of Pepto Bismol. Nevertheless, the finished product was the perfect blend of a tomato base with meat and vegetables that warmed both the stomach and heart on a cold frosty evening.

This day, however, presented one slight dilemma – there were two hog's heads yet only one black pot. Obviously, only one head could be boiled at a time. Thus, the first head was cleaned and thrust into the huge dark kettle. Four to five hours later Mama pronounced the head "done" and two men removed it and set it to cool on a wooden table next to the fire.

Though you may still be feeling a bit queasy, Samson – runt of the litter – was intrigued and inexplicably drawn to the unique aroma of a freshly boiled hog's head. While his brothers and sisters scrounged for food in other directions, this little guy decided the hog's head would be a virtual daylong feast for him! So when everyone's attention was diverted, the runt Samson hopped up, placed his paws on the wooden table, and wrestled this very large hog's head to the ground. He tugged and pulled at the fresh meat, rolling the head in the grass and dirt as he gnawed away at the goods.

Samson was well involved in his feasting before Aunt Zelma observed the little puppy chewing on this very large bovine skull, quite literally making a "pig" of himself. Grabbing a large metal spoon, she promptly chased Samson away from the head. Reluctant to leave his treasure, Aunt Old had to whack Samson a couple of times before he relinquished his feast and retreated to his hideaway beneath the house. As he made his exit, the dog left behind one seriously revolting hog's head with semi-naked bones and clenched teeth covered with a nauseating combination of grass, dirt, and assorted dog-germs.

Now, I must admit that, even on Posey Road, there are limits to the consumption of a hog's head and it took only seconds to deduce that this particular head was certainly not stew-worthy.

Next question? What was one to do with the, uh, remains. What would Miss Manners say was the proper means of disposing of one boiled, half-eaten hog's head with semi-naked bones, clenched teeth, covered with a nauseating combination of grass, dirt, and assorted dog germs?

Solution? The Posey Road pond. Two men lifted the object, loaded it onto the back of a truck, and set out for the pond located about one mile from the house.

Like a soldier on a covert operation in wartime, Samson followed the truck without being detected.

The men drove to the pond and, arriving at what they deemed the fitting site, they lifted the remains from the back of the truck and threw the hog's head into the pond with all their force. Though these were strong men, the weight of the head kept it from going very far from the edge of the pond. But, satisfied with the committal, the men returned to the task of dressing the second hog.

Meanwhile, Samson returned to his own task.

Well over an hour later, Aunt Zelma herself broke into an eerie fit of laughter. Looking up, the approximately 20 adults joined in the gawking and laughing as the meager Samson, runt of the litter, appeared at the edge of the yard, awkwardly struggling with one very large, very wet, very repulsive hog's head. With sheer "pig-headed" determination, that little dog had summoned all his strength to jump into the edge of the pond, pull the hog's head from the water, and drag it back home to complete the feast he had started earlier that afternoon. What a spectacle! The skeletal remains virtually eclipsed the tiny but determined creature that would not be deterred from enjoying his gourmet meal of freshly boiled hog's head.

Amazingly, Samson suddenly became quite popular with his five hypocritical siblings who quickly gathered around him, intent on sharing the fruits of his labor. Samson, however, seemed suddenly empowered and growled menacingly at his greedy siblings who backed away in astonishment.

No one, including Aunt Zelma, bothered Samson for the rest of the day. We left the little dog alone with his hog's head as he ate, chewed, licked and, finally, slept either from a full stomach or sheer exhaustion.

Runt of the litter, he was. He fought his way into the world and continued to fight for his place in the world. After lo these many years, I barely remember the other puppies in that litter, but I will never forget Samson. And when I think of him, I inevitably remember a tiny dog, a large hog's head, and the feast he enjoyed because of his willpower and resolve.

There are things I want just as much as Samson wanted lunch that day. There are also things I might never have if I don't somehow summon the same determination and strength that enabled Samson to achieve something far greater than anyone could ever imagine.

Lord, give me the strength to go after my own hog's head -- whatever that may be.

Cathy Lee Phillips

> *And whatsoever ye do,
> do it heartily, as to the Lord,
> and not unto men;
> Knowing that of the Lord
> ye shall receive the reward
> of the inheritance:
> for ye serve the Lord Christ.*
>
> *Colossians 3:23-24*

Jonquils in a Fruit Jar

Blossom and Stand Your Ground

The world is a sad place when you are five years old, you have no money, and your mother's birthday is two days away. To make matters worse, the little boy's mother had been sick and in bed for several days and he desperately wanted to make her feel better.

Of course, he would make her a birthday card with his box of crayons with the build-in sharpener. But he wanted to do more. His mother had been so sad recently. She did not smile anymore and she slept a lot except when awakened by a fit of coughing. Even at his young age, the boy sensed something was terribly wrong, yet he did not know what to do or say. He simply wanted his mother back and hoped a special birthday present would make her happy again.

His situation did not go unobserved by his older sister. Though separated in age by twelve years, the two were very close. They would become even closer, no doubt, as their mother's cancer advanced and the boy began to ask questions that would be hard to answer. As the "big sister" she wanted to protect the little one from the pain and uncertainty the coming days held. But she could not protect him forever and she would not be able to shield him from the anguish that would come when he learned of his mother's diagnosis.

131

"Why do you look so sad?" she asked one crisp winter afternoon. "What can I do to make you feel better?"

The five-year-old explained his wish to give his mother a wonderful birthday present that would make her happy again. But he had no money. His sister understood all too well. Since their father had left months before there had been little money for anything. Now that their mother was unable to work, they struggled to buy the basics . . . and birthday presents were not on the list of basics.

The older sister did not succeed in cheering her brother. In fact, she was more disheartened than ever.

"Let's go for a walk," she suggested. The two loved walking the fields and dirt roads surrounding their little house at the edge of the woods. Holding hands, they walked slowly down the long driveway and across the graveled road. They spoke very little as they trudged the uneven ground of last summer's vegetable garden, then turned onto an old pulpwood road that had not been traveled for years.

They walked to a small creek where water drifted slowly over huge, moss-covered rocks. It was one of their favorite spots. In fact, the older sister came here often to study, to write, or to simply enjoy the solitude. After sitting a while, they turned down a narrow pathway they had never before explored.

The two wanderers followed the trail as it curved sharply to the right and then opened into a large meadow. Stopping suddenly, the boy and his sister beheld the wondrous view that stretched before them. Jonquils! Hundreds – no, thousands – of them! They waltzed in the wind, bright and yellow, painting a dazzling picture against the deep blue winter sky. The meadow was teeming with flowers from one edge of the woods to the other. The two walked further, drawn by the sweet scent of spring that permeated the meadow.

Instinctively, the older sister picked a jonquil and held it to her face. Closing her eyes, she breathed deeply the familiar aroma of spring. Though a chill filled the air and they pulled their coats tightly around them, the sister and brother savored the miracle of that moment – the joy of spring existing amid the cold of winter.

"Mama likes jonquils," the five-year-old spoke, breaking the silence.

"Well, I think you just found her birthday present," his sister suggested.

The boy smiled for the first time in days and picked flowers until they dropped from his hands and fell in bunches onto the ground.

"I'll go get my wagon," he volunteered and ran quickly toward the house. His sister continued to gather flowers, pausing occasionally to marvel at the view and inhale the pleasing perfume. Her brother returned quickly with his wagon but, once loaded, it could barely hold the abundance of blossoms.

Returning to the house, the little boy became silent and looked up with tears in his eyes.

"We don't have anything big enough to hold all these flowers."

"We will find something," his sister promised.

The two searched the house, the closets, the smoke house, and the barn. Finally, in the musty cellar beneath the house they found a collection of fruit jars, old and dirty, used for canning fruits and vegetables years ago – sixteen jars in all. They gathered the dirty fruit jars and scrubbed each until it sparkled. Once cleaned, every jar was filled with water and an abundance of yellow flowers. The sweet scent of jonquils quickly permeated the tiny house.

"Can I take them to her now?"

The little boy was about to explode with excitement.

"I know her birthday is not for two more days, but can I take them to her now?"

He was smiling again and his sister agreed that right then would be a perfectly fine time for their mother to receive sixteen fruit jars filled with beautiful jonquils. They loaded every jar onto his wagon and pulled them into their mother's bedroom.

"Happy Birthday to you, Mama," the little boy practically shouted. His older sister stood back and watched. Waking from her sleep, their mother saw the flowers and laughed out loud.

"Where did you find these?" she asked.

"We found them in a special place and they were growing just for your birthday," the little one announced.

"I love jonquils," his mother replied. "They bloom in the winter and teach us that life goes on forever," she continued, glancing at her daughter.

The little boy placed the flowers all around the room – on the dresser top, on the bedside table, atop the sewing machine, and even on the hardwood floor.

His mother held out her arms and the five-year-old climbed into bed beside to her. Smiling, they fell asleep in each other's arms.

❖❖❖❖❖

The tradition began as simply as that. And the tradition continued as the little boy's mother battled the cancer that eventually took her life. But the little boy never forgot his mother's birthday or the ritual of the jonquils. Each winter he walked to the far pasture, picked a huge bouquet of flowers, and filled a fruit jar with the familiar yellow blossoms. Together, he and his older sister would place them on their mother's grave.

As the years passed, the older sister married and moved far away. They remained close and each year, just before their mother's birthday, would recall the year they had first found the beautiful field of jonquils. They smiled when remembering the dirty fruit jars that held those first simple bouquets that cheered their mother during her illness.

In his twenty-first year, the boy graduated from college and accepted a fine job that provided him with the money he longed for as a child. As the end of winter approached that year, he returned to the field of jonquils. The meadow was as beautiful as ever. The jonquils were thick and filled the air with the same sweet aroma he remembered as a child of five. Everything was basically the same except for the exquisite crystal vase he had tucked in the trunk of his new car.

Though his mother had been very happy with the simple fruit jars that held her flowers, the boy had always wished for something far more beautiful to hold her jonquil bouquet. Leaving his office early that day, he located an exquisite crystal vase to hold his mother's birthday flowers. Walking amid the blossoms, he selected only the tallest and most magnificent flowers. When the vase was filled, he secured it next to his briefcase in the back of his car.

He drove to the little church where his mother was buried and carefully removed the beautiful vase overflowing with brilliant yellow flowers. Locating a spigot next to the church, he filled the vase with water and positioned it squarely on the ground beside his mother's grave. He sat quietly for a moment, lost in his thoughts and memories. Then, saying a silent "good-bye," the boy walked toward his car.

As he walked, though, he looked back at the gravesite again and again. He climbed into his car, snapped the seat belt, and placed his foot on the gas pedal.

He could not leave. Something was wrong and he quickly realized exactly what it was.

Reaching into the trunk of the car, the boy removed an old fruit jar – smudged, scratched, and showing the obvious wear and tear of sixteen years. It was such an ordinary object yet far more valuable than the crystal he had purchased.

He walked back to his mother's grave and, carefully removing the brilliant jonquils from the crystal vase, he placed them into the old fruit jar. A sense of peace filled him as he realized that his mother's flowers were where they should have been all along.

Placing the flowers at the edge of her grave, he grasped the lesson he had been learning since he was a five-year-old child. He and his sister had gathered countless jonquils for their mother's birthday each winter – and she had loved every flower. Their mother, though, had never once asked for a crystal vase. She did not need to, because she already knew many important things about giving and receiving.

It isn't the package that makes a gift important – it is the spirit of love in which it is given.

As long as she lived in his heart and memory, the boy vowed that his mother would receive her jonquils – the yellow flowers that bloomed in the winter and spoke of life eternal.

And they would be wrapped each year, not in a crystal vase, but in a simple fruit jar filled with a child's greatest love.

Every good gift
and every perfect gift
is from above,
and cometh down
from the Father of lights . . .

James 1:17

The First Word And The Last Word

Love Blossoms and Has the Last Word

*E*vil had the first word on Tuesday morning, September 11, 2001. It spoke through the unimaginable acts of those who, possessing overwhelming anger coupled with an intense hatred of Americans, seized jetliners filled with unsuspecting, innocent victims. Evil screamed loudly as planes slammed into the towers of the World Trade Center, igniting fire and death. A third aircraft destroyed a section of the familiar walls of The Pentagon. Never reaching its intended target, a fourth place crashed into a field near Pittsburgh.

You know the story. You saw the devastation. You heard the cries. Evil spoke most articulately that day through fire, smoke, death, collapsed buildings, grieving citizens, and a million horrors that defied description.

Thousands of people died on the day Evil had the first word. But as Evil screamed, Love began to whisper and before that horrible day was over, Love assured us that Evil did not – *and will never* – have the last word.

And though it began as a faint whisper, at day's end Love had spoken boldly in countless ways.

- Love stood in lines, some up to eight hours long, to offer the gift of blood.
- Love held vigil with tears, candles, and flowers at memorials in the 62 countries that lost citizens and throughout the rest of the world.
- Love marched as firefighters risked – and many lost – their lives by entering 110-story towers engulfed in flames to save the lives of others.
- Love persisted as volunteer workers, weary beyond exhaustion, continued to search for survivors amid the debris and devastation.
- Love sang as elected officials blended their voices and "God Bless America" reverberated throughout the halls of government.
- Love rejoiced as an American flag found in the rubble of the Pentagon was rescued and unfurled proudly while defenders of our country wept tears of both pain and pride.
- Love reigned when, in one accord, our current and past Presidents prayed and sang songs of faith at the National Cathedral in Washington, D.C.
- Love resounded through the familiar voice of a white-haired Billy Graham who reminded us of God's love through the words of the Psalmist: *"God is our refuge and strength, an ever present help in trouble. Therefore we will not fear, though the earth give way and the mountains fall into the heart of the sea."* *(Psalm 46:1-2)*
- Love mourned through the tears of a CEO who openly grieved for 700 employees who lost their lives on five upper floors of the World Trade Center.
- Love triumphed as the President of the United States, his arm draped around a retired New York firefighter, stood

amid the destruction of New York and encouraged volunteers with his words, his presence, and his faith.

- Love unified a hurt and confused nation as we stood together to pray, sing, hug, cry, and fly the flag of freedom.
- Love rejoiced as, on that fateful day, the name of God was uttered more often than the name of Osama bin Laden.
- Love multiplied as an eight-pound baby nicknamed "Angel Hope" was born just hours after the death of her father, a firefighter whom she will never know.
- Love prevailed through the simple but precious words: *"I Love You!"* These cherished words were relayed by phones amid burning buildings and falling planes.

Love triumphed on that horrible day. Even those who faced their final moments of this life spoke Love's message. They did not talk of hurts, regrets, unfulfilled promises, anger, or resentments. An ordinary telephone or cell phone became a link through which husbands and wives, sons and daughters, gently whispered the greatest message of all: *"I love you and always will."*

I have lost a husband and I am intimately acquainted with the sting of grief. But in our final moments together, my husband and I shared Love's words and the gift of those words strengthens me to this very day. These same words, I am confident, will grant strength to those who now grieve deeply because they loved deeply.

Evil had the first word on Tuesday, September 11, 2001.

But Love had the last word.

It always will.

Love does not rejoice in iniquity,
but rejoiceth in the truth.
it beareth all things,
believeth all things,
hopeth all things,
endureth all things.
Love never fails.
And now abideth
faith, hope, and love.
But the greatest of these
is love.

I Corinthians 13: 6,7,8,13

About the Author

Award-Winning author, Cathy Lee Phillips, has written for numerous publications including Angels on Earth, Today's Christian Woman, and the Sunday School Leader for the United Methodist Publishing House. Her monthly column *"Laugh and Learn"* appears in the Wesleyan Christian Advocate, the Official News Source of the United Methodist Church in Georgia.

Silver in the Slop, Cathy's first book, has been enthusiastically received by readers of all ages. Each of Cathy's inspirational parables uses ordinary objects and events to reveal eternal truths. Her stories of the Christian faith combined with a good dose of down-home southern humor, invite the reader to chuckle while growing in the knowledge of God.

Cathy's varied background includes a Master's Degree in Christian Education, ministry on the staff of several churches in the Atlanta area, leadership in the field of business management, and a range of interesting life experiences. Church, civic, business, and educational groups throughout the Southeast have enjoyed her talents as a humorist, motivational speaker, writer, singer, and retreat leader.

Currently the President of Patchwork Press, Ltd., Cathy makes her home in Canton, Georgia. Her hobbies include singing, reading, traveling, spending time with friends, and avoiding yard work!

Cathy Lee Phillips
is available as a retreat leader, program leader,
humorist, motivational or devotional speaker,
or soloist for your church, business,
educational, or civic group.
She will be happy to assist you
in preparing programs
geared to a specific theme and
the needs of your group.

Please feel free to contact her:

Cathy Lee Phillips
Patchwork Press, Ltd.
P. O. Box 4684
Canton, Georgia 30115

E-Mail:
cathy@patchworkpress.com

Web-Site:
www.patchworkpress.com

Phone:
770-720-7988

Order Today!
from Patchwork Press, Ltd.
P. O. Box 4684
Canton, Georgia 30115
www.patchworkpress.com

<u>Gutsy Little Flowers</u>
_____ **copies @ $12.00 each =** _____

<u>Silver in the Slop and Other Surprises</u>
_____ **copies @ $ 9.95 each =** _____

Shipping and Handling Charges: _____

<u>Shipping and Handling Charges</u>

1-3 Books:	$ 2.00 per book
4-11 Books:	$ 1.50 per book
8-11 Books:	$ 1.00 per book
12 or More:	$ .50 per book

Ship To:

Name:_____

Address:_____

City:_____ State:_____ Zip:_____

Makes Checks Payable to: Patchwork Press, Ltd.
Georgia Residents Add 6% Sales Tax

This Order Form is Effective for all Orders as of 12/01/2001.